FIRST AID

For a Wounded Business

The Small Business
Survival Manual

Publishers Note

Neither the publishers nor the author are engaged in rendering professional advice or services to the individual reader. The ideas, concepts and suggestions in this book are not intended to be used as a substitute for working with licensed, trained professionals.

While the author and the publisher have made every effort to provide accurate information at the time of publication, neither the publisher nor the author assumes any responsibility or liability for changes that occur after publication.

Beautiful Media Books are available for bulk purchase upon request for the purpose of seminars, special promotions, fund raising and educational needs.

BEAUTIFUL MEDIA
5652 Kingsport Drive, NE
Atlanta, GA 30342
Visit our website at www.beautimedia.com

When your business isn't feeling so well... try a small dose of "Hope-ium!"

Kevin Weir

This book is dedicated to my loving wife, Gina, who has grounded me in my Christian faith and inspired me to reach for new heights in my life

Foreword

Do you have a "First-Aid" kit for your business? Well, you may have one now thanks to Kevin Weir and his innovative, detailed manual devised for not only surviving, but thriving, in an ever-competitive small business environment.

As Kevin reveals through his narrative, not only is it possible to turn a "sick" business around, it's actually highly do-able, because it is something he (and his team of Business Coaches) have done over and over again for all types of businesses in every category imaginable.

From the perspective of the small and medium sized business owner, nothing is more important than generating profit on a day-to-day basis. However, attaining profitability and finding ways to systemize that process is one of the most challenging issues most business owners will ever face. It's also, however, one of the simplest challenges to overcome. As long as you have a viable product or service, you're operating in a viable market, and you have the ability to "de-leverage" yourself in a way that doesn't deplete your resources or ability to operate YOU WILL SUCCEED.

Note that "simple" in this solution doesn't mean easy, and as you'll learn, getting to a point of profitability in your business and acquiring the "First Aid for a Wounded Business" definition of a successful business isn't always necessarily easy.

In the end however, that ultimate journey is satisfying, and it just may be one of the most profitable pilgrimages you'll ever make. Better yet, the best thing is that you'll learn lessons no one can ever take away from you; valuable "how to" strategies that will allow you (in the same way our coaches do for their clients) to create profit in any business you will ever own.

So don't just "sit back and enjoy" this book. Use it as a guide for pin pointing and diagnosing the "illnesses" within your company. Use it also as a guide for finding a prescription and a "cure" for what's ailing your business. In doing so, you'll have better insight into how business really works, as well as a better appreciation for coaching, the coaching process and its great potential.

Get ready to see your business in a new way, and be prepared to make the necessary changes you may have been putting off for a long time. Doing so will ultimately be a lasting source of health (and wealth!) for you and your company.

All the best,
Brad Sugars

Introduction

It all began with a conversation in the hallway. As business coaches, our job is to help businesses grow, improve, and get better using proven strategies that work for any company. However, since the economic recovery is still tenuous at best in the small-business sector, we find that our clients and prospective clients are firmly locked in a desperate survival mode rather than a well planned growth-and-improvement mode. Too many times desperate business owners come to our offices with companies that are bleeding to death, and we can't help them due to lack of resources on their part—and lack of time on ours. They walk out, and we wonder if they will join the ever-growing failed-business casualty list. Many times we know that the answer is YES!

That led to the conversation. One day, after yet another defeated business owner walked out of our office, Don, my business-development manager stepped out into the hall where I was standing and said, "Gee, it seems as though we have become an emergency room for sick businesses. When will we start seeing some healthy businesses come through the doors?" With that conversation, we realized that we were not designed to help businesses that were so far down the path of destruction that they could not be revived. So, what could be done? I started looking at business books already out on the market, and I found that they basically addressed two main types of business. The first one was the healthy business that wanted to grow and prosper. The other category consisted of brand-new, fledging businesses that were in a state of what Michael Gerber describes as an "entrepreneurial spasm" phase of just getting started. As far as I could determine, there wasn't any real resource guide available geared towards a business owner who was established but struggling and needing a step-by-step approach to save their company allowing it to live another year, month, week, or even a day. I read some fantastic books about team building, leadership, marketing, and sales, but learning motivational techniques from great leaders alone certainly wasn't going to help me keep my doors open. Yes, it could help me in the next few months, perhaps in later years, but in the meantime, I needed to find ways to survive TODAY!!!

The entire idea for "First Aid for a Wounded Business" is derived from the core concept that many business owners need a first-aid manual that will help them patch up their business wounds so they can become stable enough to survive—and eventually thrive. This book does not pretend to contain any magical secrets to make your business the greatest ever. Besides, we all know that there are no real magic bullets in business. Sheer focus, applied knowledge, and absolute determination is the real formula that will take you to the height of success you are seeking.

Let's think about this in medical terms. If you've been in an accident and you have blood pouring from your body, would you want the paramedics to start exercising your legs to make them stronger? Hardly! Yet too many business books and resources are all about "exercising" different parts of your business, while they ignore the fact that in actuality you are hemorrhaging and don't know how to bandage up your own gaping business wounds.

I want you to treat this book as your own personal survival manual. Follow along with the story and see where your business fits in with what's happening to our "patient" Eric and his team. As you proceed through the pages, I will ask you to perform some triage on your business. Where does it hurt, and why is it hurting? Once you have identified the level of seriousness of your own wounds, the next step is to take a look at the treatment options presented in the book and find the ones that need to be applied to your particular situation. In First Aid for a Wounded Business I have provided specific instances where you can prescribe treatment plans, along with information about when and how you will apply those treatment plans. Don't pretend that you can stop the bleeding simply by reading this book or through sheer knowledge alone. You will have to carefully perform the exercises in the book, and then continually do what needs to be done thereafter. Will everything I talk about in this book apply to you? Probably not. However, if you follow the pattern of the treatment plan as prescribed, you will have a much better chance of achieving a positive outcome than you would have by doing nothing, or by trying a few random shotgun strategies here and there.

Here is your opportunity not only for obtaining survival, but for achieving true success in business. However, you have to take the first step by delving deep into this book and actually dressing your own wounds. As one of my fellow coaches loves to say, "Nothing changes if nothing changes..."

Table of Contents-

Chapter

1

Shock- Living in Denial

Shock, in medical terms is your body's natural reaction to a traumatic injury. When we hurt ourselves, our bodies mask the pain that we should be experiencing in order for us to temporarily function. In short order however, the pain comes through in full force, and we have to deal with the issue. Sometimes, shock stops us from seeking medical help. The injury doesn't feel as bad as it looks. This can have deadly consequences.

Living in denial about your business problems is much like the shock effect. As a business owner your business can exhibit multiple symptoms that show your business is sick, but if you don't know how to look for and recognize those symptoms or choose not to look for them, you slide into a state of denial.

There are three main "living in denial" behaviors that business owners exhibit. The first is the "Ignorance is Bliss" behavior. "If I don't know the details about my business, then I don't have to face any problems." The second is the "Somebody else can solve that" behavior. "Yes we have a problem, but I have (insert employee's name here) working on that." The most common—and most dangerous— is "The Black Knight" form of denial. If you saw the movie Monty Python and the Holy Grail, you remember that Black Knight fights King Arthur. One by one, his limbs are hacked off. Each time the poor Black Knight loses a limb, he explains it away as "Merely a flesh wound" or "Tis but a scratch," even though he can clearly see his chopped off arms and legs lying right next to him on the ground. As a business coach, I have entered a company many times to see major negative symptoms that will lead to business failure down the road. When I point these out, typically the owner is aware of the problems, but I get an explanation that sort of parallels the old "tis-merely-a-flesh-wound," denial from the Black Knight. He wants to deal with issues that have no relation to fixing the wound which will ultimately result in allowing the business to bleed to death.

Eric

"How did I get here?" Eric asked himself as he stared down into the black, icy waters of the Columbia River. Standing on the edge of a bridge contemplating suicide is never how Eric figured his business and his life would come to an end

Eric, the 37-year-old owner of a truck repair business in Kennewick, Washington that specializes in repairing 18-wheelers, is regarded as one of the greatest truck mechanics in the Western United States. A family man with a wife and two kids in grade school, Eric learned truck repair from his dad, who had a successful 40-year career in large truck repair. By 19, Eric was well into his apprentice program, and by 25, he had become a full-fledged journeyman. His reputation as being the "Boy Genius" of the Pacific Northwest's truck repair world meant he was in constant demand for his services. Despite multiple pay raises and numerous awards he received from his employer, Eric decided at 27 to start working out of his own small facility. He witnessed the owner of the company getting rich as a result of his labor, and he saw less-than-mediocre mechanics kept around by a management team that had, in Eric's opinion, risen past their level of competency. Due to these problems, customer service had suffered, and he vowed to himself that when he started his business, it would be totally different.

Sure enough, in the first year on his own, he brought over loyal clientele from his old employer, and in short order, he was flooded with referrals from satisfied customers who spread the word of his new business venture. He was forced to move from his small, improvised facility on his property to a garage where he could provide many more services.

Shortly after the move, he realized he needed help, so he hired some of his buddies from the past employer, and hired a few more friends to perform non-technical tasks, such as parts ordering and clerical work. With these hires, the business exploded into a spasm of sky-high growth. The phone kept ringing, and the trucks kept rolling in at a pace that Eric could have never anticipated. Fortunately for him, the space next door became available, and within a few days, he knocked out walls and purchased new lifts, testing units, and tools that would allow him to double his business capacity.

As fate would have it, Eric landed a monster contract with the region's largest trucking company that would guarantee that the doubling he planned for would occur in months instead of years. It was an exhilarating thrill, and Eric couldn't believe his good fortune.

But rumblings of dissatisfaction soon followed. In the 5 years that Eric had worked to get his business going, he had stopped taking vacations, rationalizing it away by telling himself and his loved ones that this was the sacrifice he needed to make to get his business off the ground. Every year brought the promise of a vacation the next year, but it never happened. One night, his wife angrily confronted him about the broken promises, and the excessive hours spent at the facility. "I'm sick and tired of being the casual mistress to the real love of your life, your business," she exclaimed in a loud tirade. During the following months, the fights grew worse as Eric failed to attend his kids' sporting events due to a steady sequence of unforeseen surprises at the business that keep him there. He became adept at getting out of promises that he made to the family, and many nights, he'd come home after the kids had gone to bed. Soon, his children became distant. The strains in the marriage became heavier as his wife started the slow process of emotionally shutting down. Eric sensed this, yet he felt powerless to do anything about it as the business consumed virtually all of his time and his attention.

Determined to get a handle on his business, Eric hired Jessica to become his full-time bookkeeper. Jessica was a 30-year-old former bookkeeper from another trucking company several hours away. She answered the ad he placed on Craigslist, and after a short interview and a quick demonstration of her skills, she had the job. As with all of his hiring decisions, Eric used the gut-feel method. He simply hired people he liked. Shortly after she arrived, Jessica started up a romance with Reggie, the parts manager whom Eric had brought over with him from his old employer. Although Reggie was a good employee, he had a problem with alcohol, and soon enough, Jessica and Reggie were hitting the bars on a nightly basis.

Since Eric had mainly hired his friends over the years, the culture of the company became very informal and undisciplined. Eric's supervision of his employees soon became almost non-existent, and the quality of the repairs started to slide. Eric started to spend more and more hours each day fixing the mistakes his employees had made, which elevated his frustration level, along with his blood pressure. Nevertheless, he didn't want to re-train his employees because he felt it would take too long. Besides, he told himself, he didn't really spend that much time fixing all of those mistakes. In reality, he had no idea where he spent all those long hours in his business. Most days, he came in right at 7 a.m. and just kept reacting to problems until he left at 9 p.m.

As time went on, the repair times became longer and longer. Every day, Eric got a call from one or another dissatisfied client who was wondering why a truck had not been delivered as promised. Soon, clients started dropping off and cash flow became a problem. Eric then started dumping money into advertising campaigns in order to attract new customers. However, as more new customers arrived and Eric shifted his attention to these new accounts, many of the older accounts stopped doing business with him as they felt that Eric and his company no longer focused on their needs. Nevertheless, Eric forged steadfastly ahead figuring that clients would come and clients would go, so it wasn't that big of a problem.

But life got worse for Eric. He started drawing on his lines of credit with his banks and secured a second mortgage on his house in order to dump more cash into the business. The justifications just kept rolling around in his mind. "This is what it will take to make this business happen," he kept telling himself over and over again. Soon the stress started to get to him, and the best way for him to alleviate that stress was by doing what he did best and what gave him the most joy...fixing trucks. Hours upon hours were spent inside the engine compartments of his best customer's trucks, all the while the business was drifting directionless towards impending disaster.

One day while walking through the office area, he noticed an envelope on Jessica's desk. It was from the IRS. He opened up the letter and was horrified to learn that his company had failed to pay its payroll taxes for the last two quarters, and that action was in process to initiate collections in order to pay the back taxes. Digging through the desk, he discovered multiple letters from the state of Washington demanding immediate payment for unpaid worker's compensation taxes and excise taxes. Just then, Jessica entered the office, and when Eric angrily confronted her with his discovery, Jessica explained that she had tried to keep the state and IRS at bay while she "balanced out" cash-flow issues. She and Reggie took off shortly after that incident and did not return.

Sensing that something was wrong, Eric called Jake, his accountant, to conduct an audit of the company books. When Jake came in and performed his investigation, the horrible truth came out.

Jessica, with Reggie's help, had embezzled over $400,000 from the company over a three-year period. Since Eric never even looked at his financials except to sign his federal tax return once a year, he was clueless that anything like this was happening. On top of that, all of his suppliers were demanding cash on delivery for parts, which was impacting cash flow, and his next round of payroll checks coming out in a few days were going to bounce. Eric couldn't believe two employees he considered his friends had been stealing from him for so long—and so prolifically.

As Eric drove home that night, a total wave of despair overwhelmed him. His wife had finally moved out and filed for divorce several months ago, and he had not seen the kids in two months. Everything he had built in his business was just about to crumble at his feet. All hope for any success in business had been destroyed, and his mind replayed scenes of a wasted life punctuated by abject failure. He now realized that there was only one way out of this misery and despair. As he drove across the Blue Bridge, he stopped his car, got out, and stepped to the side to overlook the Columbia River and the Hydroplane Course. For a moment, he remembered hot July weekends and the happy memories he had of watching the Hydroplane races with his father as he grew up, and then taking his own kids down to the races to share with them the same experiences. However, those happy memories quickly faded away and the crushing despair once again took over. Hundreds of feet in the air, he knew that jumping into the water would mean instant death, and instant relief from the hell he had created for himself. As annoyed drivers honked their horns and swerved their cars around the traffic obstruction that Eric had created, he stepped up on the railing and prepared to jump. "So is this how it's going to end?" thought Eric to himself as he contemplated the finality of his potential decision.

Within seconds, several state patrol cars raced onto the bridge to deal with the emerging situation. The lights and commotion distracted Eric from his intended task for a moment, and as he looked over at the crowd gathering he thought to himself, "Am I really ready to do this?"

He was not ready for it to end. He was ready for a new beginning.

Chapter

2

*How Do You Know When
You're Wounded?*

The call came in at 7 a.m. that morning. The phone ringing in the home office failed to rise above the din of another typical frantic morning as the kids got ready for school, the dogs played with each other, and The Today Show blared in the background, starting with its dramatic announcement of breaking news about another political scandal.

"Dad, your phone is ringing," called out his son.

"This is a bit early for a phone call," Dr. Michael Dirkers thought to himself, but when he saw Crondolet, the local mental hospital, on the caller ID, his annoyance shifted quickly to puzzlement. This wasn't a typical call, especially for a business coach.

Dr. Mike, as he was called, had developed one of the most unusual career paths that just about anyone could take. Graduating at the top of his class from University of Washington Medical School, Dr. Mike dove headlong into his passion of becoming an emergency room physician, following in the footsteps of his legendary father, Dr. Chester Dirkers, who worked the emergency room at Sacred Heart Medical Center in Spokane, Wash., for almost 30 years. However, after six years of grinding out night after crazy night of dealing with the chaos and never-ending adrenaline rushes of life-and-death situations, Dr. Mike developed the entrepreneurial "bug" and decided to open his own urgent-care clinic. He realized quickly that he enjoyed being a business owner even more than being a physician, and during the next 10 years, he developed his creation, Inland Northwest Urgent Care into the premier urgent-care system in the region, with 13 locations in four states. Dr. Mike had achieved his dreams in business and his life, but something was missing, yet he could never quite put his finger on it, even as he continued to rack up success after success as an entrepreneur. Finally, at the age of 42, Dr. Mike met the woman of his dreams. Becky was a 37-year-old single mom and a widow whose husband died during a tour in Iraq. Becky was also a gifted counselor who had an amazing ability to read people and drill down to the real issues in their lives. Their first date, a blind date set up by mutual friends, ended up being an all-night conversation on multiple levels of their lives. The chemistry was electric, and in short order, romance blossomed. The self-professed bachelor for life had finally succumbed to love.

One night, over a meal of baked Alaskan salmon at their favorite restaurant in Spokane's quaint Browne's Addition, Becky finally brought up the topic she had wanted to talk about for months since their engagement. "Mike, what do you really want your legacy to be in life?" She had sensed from the beginning that Dr. Mike had a higher calling than just owning medical clinics, but she was never really prepared to bring up the topic until she felt secure enough in their relationship. Dr. Mike sat there, his eyes staring at a point on the teak hardwood floors of the restaurant for what seemed like an eternity. Finally he looked up slowly, stared at Becky for a few seconds, and began to relate the stories of patients in his clinics who were fellow business owners. They suffered from stress-related diseases that were far more prevalent and devastating than in those seen in other groups of people. Dr. Mike related the story of a good friend of his who owned a hardware store. Over time, his business struggles took a toll on his physical body, and at 54, he died of a stress-induced heart attack. Dr. Mike had grieved as he saw patient after patient in his clinics taken down by the stress of their businesses, many losing everything they ever had, including their lives. At that moment he knew what he needed to do.

Within a few months, Dr. Mike sold his entire chain of clinics, sold his house in Spokane and moved to Kennewick to be closer to Becky's family. He went through intense training to become a Business Coach. Starting all over again was not easy. Adjusting to his new role of being a single-person business working out of a home office and learning to be a step dad to two rambunctious grade school boys took some time. However, after a few years, Dr. Mike had developed sterling reputation in the region as "The Business Doctor," specializing in rescuing sick and wounded businesses and helping them recover so that they could become successful. His services were in high demand, and his success rates were truly amazing. However, Dr. Mike was about to encounter one of the toughest cases he had ever encountered.

The Patient

"Dr. Mike," said Crondolet psychologist Dr. Mark Johnson, "we have a patient here who attempted suicide last night. The police talked him off of the Blue Bridge, and they brought him in here last night. "

"So what does this have to do with me? " Dr Mike said.

"Yes, I know this may seem very unusual, but you have come highly recommended from some of my other colleagues who have met you in the community. It sounds like his business is falling apart, and he needs some level of help. He has agreed that once he is released from here, he would let you do a diagnostic on his business. He is still in a state of denial about his issues, so this might be a difficult case initially." Dr Johnson went into detail about what Eric had told them about his business and his life.

"How long before he is released?" Dr. Mike asked as he furiously scribbled notes in his indecipherable medical shorthand.

"At this point, it's probably going to be about a week, but he has agreed to meet you the day after he gets back to work," Dr. Johnson said.

"Great," Dr. Mike said. "I will need him to fill out a questionnaire on his business and get it back to me prior to our meeting so I can be prepared. Do you think he will be stable enough to start filling it out in the next day or two?"

"Yes, hopefully the mood stabilizers we gave him should begin to take effect within the next 24 hours," Dr. Johnson said. "I don't typically recommend patients work on questionnaires not related to their mental health, but in this case, I can see the need. Send your paperwork over and we'll get him to fill it out and send it back to you."

The Evaluation

Eric sat quietly in his office as the familiar, ever-present noise of grinders, air jacks, and diesel engines echoed through the cavernous work bays of Clearwater Truck Maintenance and Repair. The past two days in the office since returning to work had been some of the loneliest days that he had ever encountered. Not knowing what to say, the team offered their support and reassurances, but little else. Unanswered phone messages littered his desk as he prepared for his meeting with the business coach that afternoon. He felt better now, thanks to the modern wonders of mood altering drugs, but the medication had not taken away the pain of business failure that surrounded him in from every direction. The bills were still piled high, and the work that only Eric could do filled both the work bays and his office. His team went through the days in a zombie-like demeanor with no inspiration, direction, or focus.

When the business coach walked in, Eric pushed his papers to the side; hoping in doing so wouldn't make himself look as disorganized as he really was. He recognized how pathetic the attempt was and smiled meekly at the new acquaintance.

"You must be Dr. Dirkers," he said. "Hi Eric, Dr. Mike Dirkers. It's nice to meet you." Eric felt instantly intimidated by Mike's firm handshake, dark-blue power suit, and polished shoes.

"I know I don't look very good in these old overalls, but hey, at least it's better than those hospital gowns I was in last week," Eric said. "Hey, sometimes I'd love to just put on an old pair of coveralls and broken-in tennis shoes instead of dressing in this stiff suit," Mike said as he smiled and put down his briefcase. "Oh by the way, just call me Mike since we are not obviously in an emergency room." "Works for me," Eric replied as he started to feel a little less uncomfortable.

"Can I take a look around the shop?" Mike asked. "Sure, but it isn't going to be the prettiest sight," Eric said. "We've let a lot of things slide." "That's ok, just want to see what we're starting with," replied Mike.

After a tour of the shop, Eric and Mike went back to Eric's office. Mike sat down, pulled out a portfolio with a series of prepared questions, and started the meeting. "Eric, the purpose of my visit today is to do an evaluation of your business and find out what are the challenges you are facing in order to best help you get your business under control. When I was an emergency-room physician, the paramedics would bring in a patient and give us the vital signs, field treatment, and the scope of the situation. I would then do a quick evaluation of the patient, and from that evaluation determine the most appropriate treatment regimen. Likewise, I'm going to basically identify all of the wounds in your business so I know what needs to be addressed and in what order. In the ER, it doesn't make any sense to treat your broken leg if you are in the middle of a full-scale heart attack, and the same is true in business. You may have many broken legs, but let's identify your business heart attacks first, so that those can be treated in as rapidly as possible."

Mike paused, and then said, "Are you ready, Eric?" "About as ready as I would be if I was having a Colonoscopy without anesthesia, but if it's the first step to getting me and this business well, then let's do it," Eric said with a hint of both dread and hope.

OK, First of all let's talk about hours spent at work. How many hours are you spending on a daily and weekly basis?

"One sign of a wounded business is the number of hours the owner spends in the business. Now, I know that when you started your business you were probably working 75 to 85 hours per week, and that was necessary just to get the business up to speed. Correct?"

"Yep" Eric answered quickly.

"However, in a healthy business, the owner should work only when he chooses to work. One of the reasons that you start a business is to eventually give you all the time freedom you want. So after a few years, you should start seeing your time in the business go down. Remember, you should own the business, and the business should not own you."

"Yeah, I wish," Eric said. "This place owns me lock, stock, and barrel."

"Now, you started this business ten years ago from what I saw on your questionnaire you sent over, but you are still working 75 to 85 hours per week. How is that working for you?"

"It's not," Eric said with a heavy sigh. "When I started this business, it was exhilarating working all those extra hours because I was in love with my independence. Now, it crushes me to drive past baseball fields in the summer evenings where I see dads that have been home for hours and are playing with their kids, and I'm just leaving the shop for home."

Relationships at home. What is your family saying about your lifestyle?

"Well, with that note, another clear indicator that you have a wounded business is your life at home with the ones you love. The level of tension between your spouse, children and those closest to you is almost directly related to the severity of the wound to your business. The fact is, you probably drag your business problems into your home, where they fester until they blow up in an unrelenting explosion of negative emotions. Your family comments on why you never show up for your kid's school events. Maybe it's the Thanksgiving that you didn't make it home until well after the Turkey was carved, or the birthday dinner that culminated in a big fight because you kept taking business calls instead of turning off your cell phone. You've become isolated from the ones you love the most in life, and you don't know what to do anymore. Eric, does this sound like you?"

A tense quiet enveloped the office as Eric looked down and paused for what seemed like an eternity. With a small tear in his eye and a quiet quiver in his voice, Eric said, "It's like you've been reading my mail. Virtually everything you just mention has happened to me in recent years." Then he reached into his desk, pulled out a thick manila envelope, and tossed it on the desk in obvious frustration. "This is what this business has brought me," Eric exclaimed in an angry voice tinged with sadness.

"What is this?" Mike asked.

"Divorce papers from my wife. She finally gave up about 6 months ago. I haven't signed them. I don't want a divorce. I love her, and I love my kids. I want to do whatever it takes to repair the damage that I have caused by my obsession with this business. She's been pressuring me to sign this and put this to bed. I have been stalling hoping that maybe, somehow, she will reconsider. I just hope it's not too late."

"I have no idea if it's too late," Mike said. "But living in the land of regret of damaged relationships will never help you get what you want out of life. Once the business is stabilized, I hope you can work on the wounded relationships with your family."

Personal health issues. Have you gained weight, lost energy, or lost sex drive?

"Another symptom of a wounded business is your own health

issues. Study after study confirms that stress in your life contributes to all sorts of negative health issues, such as obesity, heart disease, immune deficiency, and a whole host of other health issues. In my years in the ER, I would see a high proportion of business owners who came in with chronic health issues that they would ignore for years until they would literally collapse and have to be rushed in on a stretcher."

"Well, ending up in the loony bin sure doesn't look good on my health records," Eric chuckled sadly. "I know I drink too much, and my doctor has been lecturing me for years to quit smoking and get some real exercise, but I'm sort of like the Lloyd Bridges character from the movie Airplane who kept telling everybody it was a bad day to quit whatever bad habit he was supposed to quit. Frankly, the business has given me too many excuses to continue my bad health habits," Eric exclaimed as he reached for a box of jelly donuts sitting on his desk. "Want one?"

"No thanks," Mike said, as he gave an ironic smile.

Deficit spending – Are you relying on credit cards, lines of credit, and bank loans to meet basic expenses such as payroll, suppliers, etc.?

"Next, we need to look at another very common symptom of a wounded business, and that is deficit spending. Most wounded businesses that I have encountered have almost no financial controls in the business, so there is no idea how much money is coming in and out of the business. The only solution is to perform the most basic checkbook management. If there is money in the checking account, you are happy, and when there is no money in the checking account, you are sad. You can get away with this for a while when you are a young business with low overhead, but as you grow and accumulate assets over time, it becomes imperative that you know your financial position. When cash flow suffers, it's easier to get money into the business from loans, line of credits, and credit cards instead of getting control of revenue and expenses. After awhile, you max out all the sources of funds you can find in the imaginary hope that things will magically turn around. How have things been for you in this area, Eric?"

"I've been playing credit card merry-go-round for several years," Eric said. "I keep maxing out cards, and getting new cards to cover the minimum payments on the old cards. Now, I'm getting rejected for new cards, so I'm in a real financial dilemma."

Non-returning customers. Do you have customers who disappear without a word?

"A sometimes overlooked but critically important symptom of a wounded business is loss of customers. When a business is wounded in other areas, it invariably manifests itself in less-than-adequate customer outcomes. Your service suffers. Your employees lack focus on the customers and their needs, and soon enough, the customers stop sending work your way. Here's the biggest thing you need to know; they will almost never tell you that they are leaving. They just do it. Why bother with the conflict?"

"I think I have good customer satisfaction," Eric proudly announced.

"How would you know?" Mike asked.

"I just assume that if their truck is working when it leaves the bay, that's what they're looking for."

"How long do customers stay with you?"

"I've never really tried to figure that out," Eric said. "I just know that I've got to keep getting new customers to replace the old customers."

"You know one of my favorite authors, Jeffrey Gitomer, put it best in a title to one of his books Customer Satisfaction is Worthless, Customer Loyalty is Priceless," Mike said as he waved his arms in emphasis. "Your customers vote with their dollars, and you need to know if their vote is being cast with another business."

Does employee drama happen constantly? Do good employees leave?

"Tell me about employee morale around the business in the past few years," Mike said.

"Morale? What morale?" Eric snapped. "Way too much of my time is taken up in my employee arguments, complaints, and just plain whining. I feel like my office is Grand Central Station...a parade of problems that just can't be solved by a wave of a magic wand."

Eric paused for a moment, gave a wry smile and asked, "Do you have a magic wand?"

"Don't I wish," Mike replied. "I'd make billions if I had that secret wand that I could wave over every employee and make them happy all the time and loving every second of the work day. But the fact is that employee problems are simply a symptom of a dysfunctional business rather than the cause of the dysfunction. Let me ask you Eric, how much employee turnover do you have?"

"Way too much," Eric said. "At first when I would lose a good mechanic, I really didn't worry about it because I could always go out and get another good one. I had them calling me and wanting to work here. I heard their ugly stories of abusive bosses, bad attitudes, and no pay raises in years. They practically begged me to hire them. You know what? I haven't received a call like that in the last three years. Now, it's like they just bide their time here until they can land a job with some other shop. It's discouraging. "

"Why do you think they leave?" asked Mike.

"I get a variety of reasons, but usually I'm told that they can get more money somewhere else. I just can't pay them the kind of salaries that other repair businesses can."

"That's usually just a smokescreen to justify their real reasons," Mike replied "There was a study several years ago that asked employees to rank what were the most important factor in job satisfaction. Did you know that money was only number 4 out of 10? They're telling you it's money, but they are really leaving because they want peace, fun and contentment in their jobs instead of conflict, anger and stress."

Do you return calls?

"Eric, I see that your message light is blinking. How many messages are on your voice mail?" Mike asked as he looked at Eric's phone.

"I don't know. Maybe a couple of dozen."

"Why so many?"

"I figure if I ignore my messages long enough, I won't have to deal with all the negative crap that is sitting on those messages. I just don't have the mental energy to do that."

"Do you send all your calls to voice mail?"

"Yeah, I just figure that I'll get back to them when I'm ready."

"And how long is that?"

"Maybe a few days. Who knows?"

"Probably a few weeks," Mike chimed in. Eric smiled and gave a heavy sigh as if to acknowledge that Mike was probably right.

"What if one of those messages was your best customer giving you a referral to the director of operations for the biggest trucking company in the region? How would you feel ignoring that message?"

"Well that's a pipe dream right now, but if that was the case, I guess it would suck," Eric responded as he shrugged his shoulders.

"See Eric, this is another classic dysfunction of a wounded business. You ignore important messages that you probably need to take action on, but since you want to play ostrich and stick your head in the proverbial sand, you probably miss critical actions that could save a client, get a client, or resolve a billing issue that you need to deal with."

"So this is what denial is all about," Eric uttered quietly as he stared at that constantly blinking red light. "Wow, this really sucks."

Are you staying away from friends?

"Ok, final question," Mike smiled as if to indicate that the torture was just about to end. "I noticed on your questionnaire that you indicated that you are big softball nut and have won some major softball tournaments with you team. When is the last time you played with the team?"

"Years," Eric replied as if he was growing impatient. "I just don't have the time to play softball anyway with the kind of hours I have to keep here."

"Yeah, maybe that's true," Mike responded, becoming more direct. "But I think there is also another deep-seeded reason you won't play with your buddies."

"What is that?" Eric snapped back, obviously agitated.

"You don't want to answer the tough questions your friends would ask about your business and how it's going," Mike answered with complete confidence. "You put off this false aura of confidence and success. You want to impress your friends with how good things are going in your business. The fact is, you can't lie to them anymore about your struggles. So instead of admitting the truth you just find it easier to avoid them and stay in your own cocoon of depression and despair. Isn't that true, Eric?"

Eric paused for a second, looked and Mike, and shook his head.

"You've nailed me." Eric sadly agreed. "I don't think I've ever had anyone in my life slice and dice my business and my abilities as a business owner like you have."

"There is no condemnation here," Mike replied as he softened his tone. "I'm here to help. But in order to help you, both you and I have to recognize all of the symptoms that are exhibited in your wounded business. Do you want me to help you, Eric?"

"Do I have a choice?"

"I guess you do," Mike replied. "You can keep doing what you have been doing for years, or you can have me help you get this business stabilized and moving in the right direction. Remember this, nothing changes if nothing changes."

"Well, I guess I'll see you here next Tuesday."

Chapter

3

Bleeding- Dressing Your Financial Wounds

Mike showed up on Tuesday at 8 a.m. ready to get to work. Eric greeted him as he came into the shop, and they went directly to his office. Eric had actually cleaned off his desk in anticipation of Mike's visit and was eager to get down to business. For the first time in years, Eric had some spring in his step and a level of hope in his demeanor. Mike sat down across the desk from Eric and opened his briefcase to pull out a whole bunch of forms with blocks to fill in numbers.

"Eric, today we are going to start out with how to stop your bleeding by dressing your financial wounds. Business owners who are in trouble always ask me, 'I have so many problems, where do I start?' Although there is a case to be made for starting in other areas, the fact is that the fastest way a business dies is from its financial problems...its wounds. It's sort of like a person who is hurt. You may have multiple injuries from an accident, but if I don't stop the bleeding first and foremost, then everything else is a moot point."

"Yep, makes sense," Eric replied. "So where do we start?"

Can you be saved? When to know when you need to let the patient (i.e. your business) die?

"The first thing we have to look at is if your business can be saved in the first place. As painful as it may seem, sometimes we just have to admit from the start that no matter what happens, the business is doomed and we need to bring a bankruptcy attorney to start the liquidation process. There were many situations over the years when patients came into the ER who had been clinically dead too long to consider resuscitation. Instead of taking heroic measures to try to revive them, we had to quickly ascertain that they had passed away and let the family know."

"So, what do you look for in a business that needs to die quickly?" Eric asked.

1.   Is your business in a stagnant or dying industry? The first thing we have to look at is, are you in an industry that doesn't have a future. For example, if you had a wounded business back in the 1950s making vacuum tubes

for radios, you would have almost no hope of competing against the transistor radio. Unless you could retool into a different industry, you just need to pull the plug.

    2.   Are your debts too crushing to overcome? We have to look at what you owe to whom. Sometimes, we must conclude that no matter how fast you could grow revenue and cut expenses, you would be better off ending the business. There's no use in pouring additional time and money into the business if there is just no hope of ever recovering.

    3.   Will your creditors negotiate with you in good faith, or are they going to demand liquidation? Sometimes, your creditors just won't let you restructure your debt. Perhaps they have lost confidence in you, your business, and your ability to recover. Perhaps you have burned too many bridges with them through broken promises and lack of integrity. At some point, the majority of them may feel it's in their best interest to take their chances in a bankruptcy proceeding rather than hope that you will make it.

"Do you think I will make it?" Eric asked nervously.

"Yes I do," Mike cheerfully replied. "You are still in a stable industry as trucking is still a vital transportation need in today's society. Your debts are not so great that you cannot grow your business and reduce expenses in order to pay them off in a reasonable time, and your creditors are willing to restructure your debt without putting you out of business."

What is your break even in business? Nothing is more important than this concept.

Next, we need to look carefully at what the break-even point is in your business. If we don't know where that is, then how do we know what to shoot for financially to get you moving forward?

"OK, this may seem like a dumb question, but what is a break-even point?" Eric asked.

"No dumb questions here," Mike replied with a smile. "A break-even point is the place where your total revenues cover all your fixed and variable costs for that period of time. If you have any revenue above the break-even point, you are making profit."

"What would be fixed costs and what would be variable costs in my business?" Eric inquired.

"In simple terms, variable costs are those costs that it takes to accomplish a particular job. So if you are producing a widget, it would be the cost of the raw materials it would take to make the widget and the labor necessary to produce it. In your case, Eric, it would be the costs of parts and supplies you need to buy in order to fix the trucks and your repair technician's labor costs in order to get that job done. On the other hand, fixed costs are expenses you have to pay on an on-going basis whether there are any jobs sitting the shop or not. So for example, your rent would be a fixed cost, as would be your insurance, telephone, subscription services, payments on loan, and a few others."

"Your fees would be a fixed cost," Eric chimed in.

"You got it," Mike continued. "Anything that helps to keep the place running."

"But what about those costs that seem to be both fixed and variable, like the electric bill?" Eric asked. "It's always higher in our peak season."

"That's what we call a mixed variable, but for fixing a wounded business, we are going to keep it simple and focus on categorizing expenses as either fixed or variable."

"So how do I calculate my breakeven point?" Eric asked

"Here is a simple formula: Break even equals fixed costs divided by gross margin," Mike said. "For example, in your business, we know that on a monthly basis you have $100,000 in fixed costs."

"Yes," Eric said, having worked on his financials and done some basic bookkeeping earlier in the week.

"And after your parts and your mechanics wages, you have

about 40 percent left over to cover your fixed costs and profit, so your gross margin is 40 percent."

"Ha, what profit?" Eric laughed

Mike smiled and continued, "So let's look at how the equation works in your business: $100,000 divided by 0.4 equals a $250,000 monthly break even."

"OK, so that is how much revenue I need to bring in monthly in order to pay all my bills, so I guess that means that if I'm open 22 days in a month, I need to bring in, let's see, $11,363.64 a day," Eric exclaimed as his desk calculator spit out the tape that showed the figure. "Hmmm, that sure makes planning a lot easier knowing this. Ok, what's next?"

FORMULA:

Total sales - Deduct materials and labor = Gross Profit

$$\frac{\text{Fixed costs}}{\text{Gross Profit}} \quad = \quad \text{Break Even}$$

EXAMPLE:

$$\frac{\$100,000 \text{ fixed costs}}{0.4 \text{ gross profit}} \quad = \quad \$250,000 \text{ break even}$$

$$\frac{\$250,000 \text{ break even}}{22 \text{ days open for business}} \quad = \quad \$11,363.64 \text{ required daily income to break even}$$

Deal with your tax issues immediately.

"Now it's time to start tackling your back-taxes issues. One of the fastest ways that you can lose your business is to ignore late and unpaid tax liabilities you have to local, state, and federal taxing authorities. I've seen lots of business owners do the ostrich routine and stick their heads in the ground hoping that their tax issues would just go away. Either that or they keep making promises they know they can never fulfill. Pretty soon, they show up at work with padlocks on the doors and an official notice to shut down."

"I know," Eric shuttered. "I keep getting letters from both the Internal Revenue Service and the State Department of Revenue asking for lots of money I just don't have, and a constant barrage of threats to close down my business."

"Are you trying to negotiate with them yourself?" Mike asked

"Well of course, who else is going to do it?" Eric said as he gave a confused look to what was apparently a confusing question to him.

"Eric, you should never negotiate or represent yourself with tax authorities when you have the size of tax debts that you currently have."

"What do you mean?" Eric asked with obvious concern in his voice.

"Eric, state and federal tax authorities have one objective and one objective only; to maximize the amount of money they can extract from you before you shut down your business. They are skilled at using every legal, financial, and psychological maneuver in the book to get you to pay up no matter how damaging it would be to your wounded business. You do not have the same equivalent training. It's sort of like putting a 12-year-old boy in a fight with a heavyweight boxer. It's a total mismatch."

"So what do I do?" Eric asked

"Hire an enrolled agent," Mike answered.

"What is an enrolled agent?"

"An enrolled agent is an accountant who is trained and certified to represent you, the taxpayer and business owner, in front of the state and federal tax agencies who are attempting to collect on their debts. They know the ins and outs of tax law, and know how to work with the various agencies in order help you get the best deal so you can continue to operate. Imagine being accused of murder and going to trial without an attorney. Of course you'd never do it, so why would try to be your own counsel in front of people who want to take you down?"

"Yeah, but it sounds expensive," Eric said. "I'm already spread so thin financially that I can barely make payroll. And now you want me to add an additional expense?"

"And if you don't invest in an enrolled agent, you may never have any more payrolls to pay out because every dime will be going to pay your taxes. Do you really want that?"

"No," Eric sighed as he paused for a minute, deep in thought. "So how do I find one of these enrolled agents?"

Go to the website for The National Association of Enrolled Agents at www.naea.org. There, you can find a directory of agents in the area. Can you make some calls and find one this week that will start representing you?"

"Can do," Eric said.

"Ok, now it's time to look at taking action in our next area."

Turn your accounts receivable into cash coming through the door.

"Eric, let's look at your accounts receivables and their current status."

"Let's not," Eric responded sarcastically, knowing that this would be an embarrassing area he really didn't want to deal with.

"One of the fastest ways we can dress your financial wounds is by getting your customers to pay what they owe. How long have you known that you had this size of accounts receivable?"

"For a long time," Eric lamented. "But I just never knew what appropriate amount of accounts receivable I should be ok with in my business."

"What are the terms that you are offering your customers right now?" Mike asked

"Net 30 days," Eric answered. "But I'm sure there are lots of accounts that go past 30 days."

"Why is that?" Mike asked

"I know that in hard times many of my customers just can't pay me on time, so I become the nice guy and let them slide on their payments hoping that I can keep them as customers. I figure that if I don't demand payments that they will keep bringing their trucks in to get fixed, and eventually I'd get my money."

"Eric, do you realize that your customers are using you as their bank?" Mike explained as he became visibly animated. "Basically, they are taking out an interest-free loan on your business and paying you back when they feel like it. Don't you think it's time to stop that and get paid for what you do?"

"Yeah, you're right," Eric said with a hint of dejection in his voice. "But what do I do right now? I don't have time to mail out statements and wait for them to mail out the checks."

"It's time for Dialing for Dollars," Mike exclaimed. "It will be one of your primary jobs this week to pick up the phone, call each one of your accounts, starting with the highest balances in the 90-plus days category and start asking for payments. Get them to give you a credit-card number if you can't get a check from them. Next, arrange for an aggressive payment schedule, and then document it in a signed agreement you exchange with them. If they can pay you that day, send one of your guys over for the check. Develop a script that you will use when you call them so that you are not trying to do this off the cuff."

"But what if I piss off my customers?" Eric asked. "Then I just drive them to my competition."

"Eric, do you really want customers that don't pay you?" Mike said looking a little perturbed. "There is a grading system I want you to use with your customers later, but for right now, you want to get rid of customers who just won't pay you. Let them not pay your competition, and see how long that relationship lasts."

"Ok, I see your point," Eric said. "But a lot of these guys are my friends, and it's going to feel really awkward to start asking for more money from them."

"Eric, let me be blunt here. Do you own a business or do you own a charity?" Mike said obviously becoming agitated with the responses he was getting from Eric.

"I own a business," Eric meekly responded. "I guess what're telling me is that for the past several years I've treated it like a charity to make me feel better."

"That's right," Mike said obviously relieved that Eric was finally getting it. "So will you start your Dialing for Dollars campaign this week?"

"Yes, I will," Eric said. "But how can I know when I have too much accounts receivable sitting on my books?"

"That's simple," Mike said. "We will use a formula called Days Sales Outstanding."

"What's that?" Eric asked in a puzzled voice.

"It measures on average how long it takes your customers to pay you," Mike explained. "Since your terms are Net 30, you want your Days Sales Outstanding to be as close to 30 days as possible. Let me show you the formula: Annual revenue divided by 365 days equals daily revenues. Total current account receivable divided by daily revenues equals days sales outstanding.

"So let's see how this calculates out for your business. Your revenue for the last 12 months was $3 million, and your current Accounts Receivable is $500,000. So the formula in your case would be: $3 million divided by 365 Days is $8,219.18 daily revenues. Then $500,000 divided by $8,219.18 is 60.83 days sales outstanding.

"So it's taking my customers an average of almost 61 days to pay me?" Eric said with a bit of shock in his voice. "No wonder I never seem to have enough cash to pay for anything around here."

"That's right," Mike said "And in the future, we are going to put systems in place so your customers pay on time, but for right now, we have one task in this area, and that is picking up the phone and getting people to pay you now!"

"Guess I know what I will be doing tomorrow and it's not playing Mr. Nice Guy with my slow paying customers," Eric said, finally with a bit of gusto in his voice.

"OK Eric, let's go take a walk around the shop, because I want to show you another vital strategy that we will need to execute in order to bandage up the financial wounds in your business," Mike said as he opened Eric's office door and began walking out into the shop.

"I think I know where this is going," Eric said with some hesitancy in his voice.

Sell off excess inventory

Mike made a beeline for Eric's parts room, which was really more like a mini warehouse full of shelves stacked with parts that had been bought over the years. It was apparent that organization was lacking, and many of the parts had a light layer of dust that had accumulated on them over the years.

"Eric, let's take a look at your parts inventory here," Mike stated as he gazed over what seemed like an endless supply of items for virtually truck ever made. "It seems to me that you have a huge amount of inventory. Why so many parts?"

"Since I service so many different types of trucks, I need to be at the ready with a part so I don't get caught short," Eric explained, figuring that Mike didn't really understand the nuances of the truck repair business.

"Yes, but how many of these parts have been sitting on these shelves for more than two years just waiting for that future truck to come in that will need the part?" Mike asked.

"Lots of them I guess," Eric answered, "but it makes me feel good that I can just reach in and get a part when I need it without having to go out to an outside supply warehouse. Besides, I got a good deal on a lot of these parts, especially when I bought them in volume."

"Ok, so here is what I want you to do," Mike stated as he waved his hands towards the shelves as if he was waving a wand. "I want you to imagine that each one of these parts has a $1 bill attached to it, and that it's the job of each dollar bill to actively produce results for your business. How hard do you think those dollar bills are working for you right now?"

"Not very hard," Eric said as his eyes fixed on some old pieces he barely recognized. "I guess it would be sort of like a bank where you earn no interest on your money, but you keep putting in more money hoping the bank will change its mind and pay you interest."

"Right! And think about this Eric," Mike explained, "Wine gets better with age, inventory does not. Much of this inventory will be obsolete in a few years as technology advances and makes much of what you see here second rate. Even if you did buy some of this inventory at a volume discount, that discount will pale in comparison to what it costs you to store all of it. It's sort of like that bank that doesn't give you interest on your deposits, and it also gradually devalues your money over time. Not a pretty picture."

"Ok, I understand the concept," Eric said as he nodded his head. "Now what?"

"Time to go through all of this stuff and figure out what you can sell quickly and turn it into cash," Mike explained.

"Yeah, but a lot of this stuff I paid some good money for, and I can't sell it unless I sell it dirt-cheap," Eric said as he pointed at the old inventory. "For example, I paid over $5,000 for this inventory 5 years ago, and I'm sure all I could get for it is about $1,000 today. That just doesn't seem right."

"Yes, and if you wait another two to three years, this inventory will probably sell for about $500, if that. Remember, wine gets better with age. Inventory does not," Mike exclaimed. "Let's put some cash in your bank account now where it can be used rather than on a shelf where it can't be used."

"So maybe it's time for a big giant garage sale to sell off as much as I can," Eric stated as he started thinking. "That may take some time, but perhaps I take some pictures of some of this stuff, post it on Craigslist, and sell it yet this week."

"Now you're thinking," Mike said as he smiled, realizing that Eric was starting to get the picture.   "How soon could you have a complete liquidation sale?"

"Give me a few weeks, but I know there would be lots of guys here who would scoop up some if this stuff," Eric said as he calculated in his mind how much cash was really sitting on his shelves.

"Now it's time to address probably the most difficult aspect of bandaging up your financial wounds," Mike stated as he headed back to Eric's office.

"What would that be?" Eric asked inquisitively.

Get rid of non-performing staff

"Eric, I want you to take a look on your shop floor, what do you see?" Mike asked as he gazed out into the vast spaces of Eric's repair facility.

Um, not sure, lots of trucks that are being worked on or waiting to be fixed?" Eric answered wondering if this was a trick question.

"Do you know what I see?" Mike replied. "I see lots of employees, and many of them don't seem to be doing much work. Ever since I first set foot in this facility, I sense that many of your employees are not working to their full potential and are half-stepping it out there. I see lots of smoke breaks, lots of jaw-jacking, and not a lot of focus on getting the work done."

"Yeah, I've noticed that too," Eric said as he glanced over at a group of mechanics that were obviously engaged in conversation not related to work. "But since it has slowed down over the past few years, there hasn't been enough work to keep them occupied."

"So why haven't you laid some of them off?" Mike asked with a confused look on his face.

"Well I have laid off a few," Eric answered, "but I don't want to get caught short once it gets busy again."

"Eric, since you are bleeding to death financially, one of the most important things you must do is to get rid of non-performing team members. You must cut your excess payroll down in order to control your expenses," Mike said with exasperation.

"But Mike, you don't understand," Eric went on with some passion in his voice. "These men have families to feed and bills to pay, and I just can't let them go, especially with the loyalty that many of them have shown over the years."

"Eric, let me ask you again, do you own a business or do you own a charity?"

"Ok, you know the answer. So what?" Eric snapped back in a very defensive tone.

"If you own a business, it is your responsibility to make sure it survives so that the remaining employees can keep their jobs," Mike shot back. "Wouldn't it be better to lay off a few team members so that the remaining ones can keep their jobs and the business continues on?"

"Ok, I get it," Eric answered obviously uncomfortable with the idea of letting anyone go. "But how do I know how many to keep and how many to lay off?"

"First of all, let's start off with a simple financial formula called a productivity ratio. It is basically how much total financial output you produce per employee in your business, and the formula looks like this; total annual sales divided by total number of employees equals sales per employee. How many employees do you have currently have on your team?"

"Including myself, 37 full-time employees and one part-time employee in the paint shop," Eric answered as he made sure his numbers were correct.

"Ok, so in your case $3 million divided by 37.5 employees equals $80,000 in sales per employee annually."

"So is that good or not so good?" Eric asked

"Really, for your industry, you should be over $110,000 in sales per employee, so in reality, if we did the math, $3 million divided by $110,000 equals 27.3 employees."

"So I need to lay off 10 employees?" Eric asked, shocked at that large of a number.

$$\frac{\text{Total annual sales}}{\text{Total number employees}} = \text{average sales per employee}$$

$$\frac{\$3,000,000}{37.5} = \$80,000$$

Use industry standards to calculate

$$\frac{\$3,000,000 \text{ industry average sales}}{\$110,000 \text{ Industry Ave. Sales/employee}} = 27.3 \text{ Employees}$$

"That may very well be the case," Mike answered. "You will need to look at this more closely to determine who and how many to let go, and then reconfigure your teams. However, in the end, you must cut the fat out of your payroll."

"You do know that what you are asking me will potentially devastate up to 10 families in this community," Eric stated with reluctance in his voice.

"And you do know that if you don't do this, all 37 families will be devastated shortly thereafter," Mike said as he pointed out towards the shop floor.

"Ok, so what's next?" Eric said as the enormity of the task ahead of him unfolded in his mind.

Start putting a financial plan together. Budget.

"It's also time to start putting a plan on how we are going to spend our money, or in other words, a budget."

"Ooooh, the dreaded B word," Eric quipped. "I guess my spending plan has always been that as long as I have money in my checking account, I'm happy, and when I don't, I'm sad."

"Well, one of the key components of dressing your financial wounds is to figure out how much you should be spending on a weekly, monthly, and annual basis in all categories of your business."
"Ok, but where do I start?" Eric asked

"When putting a budget together, you always want to begin with the end in mind," Mike answered.

"What do you mean by that?"

"What I mean is that you need to plan for a profit in your business. In other words, you determine how much profit you want to make out of your business and develop the budget around meeting that goal. Too many business owners who develop a budget just plug in last year's sales numbers, figure out how much they spent, make a few minor adjustments, and then hope, wish, and pray that they come out with a positive profit number."

"In other words, I'm creating a financial goal for myself, and what I need to achieve financially to make that happen instead of just guessing what is going to happen and making up some random numbers," Eric answered.

"You got it," Mike replied. "I have some budgeting resources I can give you including spreadsheets, or you can go on line and find some great resources. That is the beauty of the Internet. It is full of information and tools that you can use for projects like this."

"Ok, I can get started on that," Eric responded, "but there are some major questions I will need to have answered as I create my budget."

What you should cut and NOT cut out of your expenses?

"I know that not all expenses are created equal," Eric said, "but I'm not quite sure what those are."

"Ok, so let's take a look at these and discuss the most obvious places to cut in your budget."

Where to cut

Excess payroll: Overstaffing can kill your business.

Inventory purchases: Buy only what you need when you need it. This is not the time to stock up on specials.

Rent: Is your facility too big for your needs? Maybe it's time to renegotiate your lease or move to a smaller, more efficient location.

Capital equipment: Do you really need to buy that shiny, new piece of equipment? You could just put some maintenance into your current equipment.

Insurance: Have you had an insurance professional evaluate your expenditures recently? You could be paying out thousands of dollars in unnecessary insurance policies. Find a good agent who knows your industry.

Travel: Do your people really need to stay in that five-star resort when they are on the road? Look at the trips that are made and ask yourself if they are really necessary.

Office Supplies: Are you using too much ink in your printers? Can you find an on-line source to buy your supplies at a lower cost instead of running down to the local office supply store?

Telephones: Take a look at your phone bill. Are you being overcharged? Maybe it's time to get some quotes from alternative sources such as cable or VoIP (Voice over Internet) instead of just sticking to your usual provider.

Where not to cut

Marketing: Yes, you should stop spending on marketing that does not work. However, you should never just stop marketing. Your prospects need to find you, and cutting off your marketing tells them that you are starting to fade away. That's not a good message to send out.

Sales staff: The bad ones need to go, but never get rid of a profitable salesperson just because you need to save a few bucks.

Technology: Good technology purchases are designed to make you more productive at overall lower costs. Putting off hardware and software upgrades will jeopardize your ability to improve efficiency and overall quality.

Equipment maintenance: That $300 service on a piece of equipment that you don't think you can afford right now may be what stops that $3,000 repair bill from happening a few months down the road.

Training and development: This is typically the first place a business uses to cut expenditures, and really it should be the very last place to cut. Your most valuable resource in your business is people, and if you fail to develop them, their skills can be compromised over time. Skills workshops, business coaches, and training programs keep your people sharp and ready to handle any challenge that faces them now and in the future.

"Ok, this makes sense," Eric said as he went over the list with Mike.

"Now Eric, there is one more area we need to look at when dressing your financial wounds, and you many not like to talk about this. I know I'm meddling, but it has to be dealt with."

"What's that?" Eric asked with obvious concern.

What about your personal finances? Are you draining too much money personally out of the business?

"Eric, it seems to me that you have been taking too much personal money out of your business over the past several years. Why is that?"

"I guess with all the stress that has been going on in the business, I figured that I deserved some nice things at home to compensate for all those problems," Eric said with a touch of defensiveness in his voice.

"That may be true, but the fact is that you, like many other business owners, have treated your business as a big, giant ATM machine, pulling out money whenever you felt like it. I've counseled many business owners who are ready to declare bankruptcy in their business but want to maintain a lavish lifestyle that is unsustainable.

The fact is, sometimes you just have to tell yourself and your family no to that extra vehicle, vacation home, or boat until the business can truly give it to you."

"So are you suggesting that I sell off some of my toys? Like my 44-foot Bayliner boat down at the Kennewick Yacht Club and my antique gun collection?" Eric asked.

"If that's what it takes to get control of your personal finances, then yes," Mike responded. "Think about this, if you're going to ask your business and your team to make sacrifices, and you won't, what kind of message does that sends to them?"

"I get it," Eric said, "but I will miss those parties on the river during the summer."

"Ok, so let's recap what you will get done on dressing your financial wounds before our next meeting" Mike stated as he started taking notes in his file.

Eric began to list them:

1. Determine if my business can be saved. Look at my industry, debts, and creditors to see if I can keep going.
2. Figure out where my break even is on a daily, weekly, monthly, and annual basis.
3. Find an enrolled agent to help me deal with my tax issues.
4. Start Dialing For Dollars to get my customers to pay me.
5. Sell off as much excessive inventory as possible through online sources and prepare for a big liquidation sale.
6. Lay off non-performing employees and reorganize my team.
7. Put together a budget for the business.
8. Sell my yacht and get personal finances under control.

Now it's your turn. List all of the things that you need to do in your business to dress your financial wounds. Your business may be different than Eric's truck-repair company, so your challenges will be unique to you. Put down what you will do, when you will do it, and who will help you accomplish the task.

Task	By When	Who Will help you
1.		
2.		
3.		
4.		
5.		
6.		
7.		
8.		
9.		
10.		
12.		
13.		
14.		
15.		

Chapter

4

*Pressure- Unclogging the
Blocked Arteries of Time*

It was 8 a.m. another Tuesday when once again Mike strolled into Clearwater Truck Maintenance and Repair to begin his work with Eric. Several weeks had passed, and in that time Eric had completed all of the tasks on his list in order to dress his financial wounds. Numerous phone coaching sessions had occurred where Mike and Eric discussed the specifics for the strategies as they were implemented, and finally after hours and hours of work, the business was at last able to put a halt to its financial bleeding.

Eric was sitting in his office, obviously pleased with himself about what had been accomplished, but looking disheveled and exhausted. Bags were under his eyes, and scattered boxes of take-out Chinese littered the desks as the lingering smell of day-old Kung Pao beef permeated the office atmosphere. Eric's hair had the telltale look from several days of severe bed head, and his clothes had obviously been slept in the night before.

"Good Morning, Eric. I love the smell of Chinese food in the morning. It smells like … progress," Mike said with a big smile on his face.

"Very funny." Eric snickered as Mike made light of Eric's favorite movie of all time. "I'm sure if Kurtz looked at this office, he'd say, 'The Horror. The Horror,'" Eric chuckled as he recited his favorite line from Apocalypse Now.

"Congratulations on getting most of your financial wounds dressed. It sure must feel good," Mike said with his usual cheeriness.

"Yes it does," Eric said with a smile, "but I'd enjoy it more if I was getting some real sleep at night. This place is just draining me."

"Eric, how many hours are you putting in on a daily basis right now?" Mike asked.

"Well, I haven't really kept track. I usually get here about 6 in the morning and leave around 9 at night. On Saturday, I try to keep it down to 8 hours."

"And Sunday?" Mike asked.

"I stay at home that day, but usually I'm too tired to really do anything except veg out and watch football all day long."

"Ok, so now you're seeing that the next stage in applying first aid to your wounded business is dealing with your time issues," Mike said as he reached into his briefcase to pull out his notepad and some forms.

"What's the medical angle at this stage?" Eric asked knowing that he might as well ask.

"If money and finances are the blood of your business, time is the heart and circulatory system. Think of the Coronary Arteries that feed your heart with oxygenated blood. If your arteries become constricted or blocked because of plaque, you will end up with heart attack. When your time becomes constricted in your business, you can't work effectively on your business. Therefore, the lifeblood of your business starts to dry up. Our job is to find ways to unblock your clogged arteries of time."

"So, what you are saying is that I have some bad time habits that have the same effect cholesterol has on an Coronary Artery. Bad time habits block my success?" Eric asked mustering up as much medical knowledge as possible to at least sound intelligent.

"You got the idea," Mike answered.

"OK, so where do we begin?" Eric answered with more enthusiasm than he had at the start of the last session.

Where are you wasting time in your day?

"The first thing we need to do is establish exactly what you do on a daily basis to determine which things are productive and which are time wasters," Mike explained.

"I guess I just don't see how I could be wasting any of my time," Eric answered as he shrugged his shoulders. "As soon as I walk in the door of this place, I am going as fast as I can. I'm probably the hardest working person in this facility."

"That's right," Mike exclaimed emphatically. "But the question is, are you working harder, or should you be working smarter?"

"I'm not sure where you are going with this," Eric said with a puzzled look on his face.

"Let's start off with a quick study of your time. How many hours a week do you work in your business?" Mike explained as he put his form in front of Eric and gave him a pencil.

"Well, let's see. It's going to be different for different weeks, but I guess I will write down what is the average," Eric pondered as he started to put the pencil on the form:

Monday: 14 hours

Tuesday: 14 hours

Wednesday: 16 hours

Thursday: 12 hours

Friday: 11 hours

Saturday: 8 hours

Total: 75 hours

"Ok, now I want you to write down all the tasks you perform on a weekly basis and how many hours you spend doing them. So in other words, how many hours you spend in bookkeeping, sales, working on the trucks, parts ordering, personnel issues, and anything else you can think of."

Eric thought for a minute and then started filling out the form:

Working on trucks: 32 hours

Organizing and setting up tools: 3 hours

Bookkeeping: 8 hours

Meeting with customers: 4 hours

Running deposits to the bank: 2 hours

Ordering parts and supplies: 4 hours

Filling out paperwork: 4 hours

Meetings with employees and managers: 4 hours

Responding to e-mails: 6 hours

Total= 67 Hours

"Hmmm, somehow I can't account for 8 hours," Eric said as he looked at the two columns and shook his head. "So what does this mean, Mike?"

"It means one of three things: you missed some of the activities that you're doing and forgot to include them in the task list; you have underestimated how long you work on a particular activity, or you have 8 hours that you just fritter away," Mike explained as he looked at Eric's task list.

Eric scrutinized the sheet, sat back for a few minutes to think how his typical days go by, and then started to scratch out some figures and began to write some items on the 2nd column.

"I know that the 75 hours I work is probably pretty accurate," Eric explained as he looked as his desk calendar. "However, I just realized I spend about 3 hours a week just cruising the Internet, and at least another 3 hours jaw-jacking with some of the guys after they get off shift. I spend a total of 10 hours on e-mails, so that probably accounts for those 8 hours."

"So now we know that 6 hours of your time is just completely wasted," Mike said as he looked at the form.

"Probably true," Eric said as he nodded. "But I don't get why that's such a big deal?"

"Think about this, Eric. You can always make more money, but you can't make more time. Money is not the limited resource in life. It's time," Mike said as he pointed to Eric's calendar on the wall.

"Maybe I don't quite understand Mike; do you have an example of this concept?" Eric asked as he obviously struggled to understand where Mike was going with this concept.

"Ok, let's put this in simple terms. How many hours do you have in a day?" Mike asked.

"24."

"And how many hours does Bill Gates have in a day?"

"24"

"And what is the difference between you and him?"

"Billions," Eric exclaimed as a big smile came across his face.

"Do you think Bill Gates learned to use his time effectively to help him earn those billions?" Mike asked.

"Yeah, I can see where you're going with this," Eric said as he finally started to understand. "I've probably wasted a lot of time over the years doing things that didn't make me an extra dollar."

"Ok, so now you know you have identified a few obvious time wasters that you can eliminate that will free up some more of your time. Next it's time to look at what is one of your biggest issues that you have with time."

Are you a control freak? Is this preventing you from using time wisely?

"Ok Eric, let's go back to your time study. What I want you to do now is to find at least two activity areas that you can start delegating to other people on your team, or develop a system so that you can start freeing up some of your time," Mike said as he looked at Eric's time exercise.

"I just don't see anything in this list here that I can delegate to anybody," Eric explained as he also looked at the time-study exercise.

"Why not?" Mike asked.

"Well, let's see," Eric said as he went down the list one by one. "There are a number of customers who only want me working on their trucks, so that work can't be delegated. I'm not about to give over control of the bookkeeping so I won't be ripped off again, which goes along with running deposits to the bank. I'm the only one who the customers want to talk with. I know what parts need to be ordered so I can't delegate that either, and since the paperwork has to be filled out correctly, I'm the only one who can do that. Obviously, I have to respond to my own e-mails, so when it comes right down to it, there is just nothing here I can really delegate to anyone else," Eric said as pounded his finger on the time-study form. "I know that if something is going to be done right, then I've got to do it myself."

"You know what one of your biggest problems is?" Mike said as he glared at Eric.

"No."

"You are a control freak! And the fact is you are not alone in this problem. Almost every client I work with who has a wounded business suffers from this affliction," Mike said with an emphasis that Eric had never seen up to this point.

"Explain," Eric said somewhat taken aback.

"You have a firm belief that since you are the best at a task, that only you can be doing it. You have a fear that if you let go of a task, that someone will mess it up and hurt your business. And since this is exactly what has happened in your business, you then clutch tighter and tighter to that task, thereby forcing you to work the outrageous amount of hours you currently work."
"How true, but if I'm the best at a task, why would I be so fool-

ish as to give it up to someone else who can't do it half as good as I do?" Eric asked.

"Because you need to stop being good at doing $10-an-hour tasks, and become an expert at doing $100-an-hour tasks," Mike said.

"How's that?" Eric asked

"Let me give you a story to explain this," Mike said as he pulled out another time study sheet that was already filled out and showed it to Eric. "Fred was a client who owned a roofing company and had virtually the same business problems that you have encountered. When I did his time study with him, I discovered he was spending about 15 hours a week running roofing supplies out to the crews. They would call him up on his cell phone explaining that they were short supplies, so he would hop into his truck, go to the supply warehouse, purchase the materials, and run them out to the site. I asked him, 'Fred, how much would it cost you to hire a person to run those supplies out to the job sites?' He figured that with labor, taxes, cell phone, and extra insurance, it would cost him about $17 an hour. I then asked him, 'Fred, how much money do you make doing bids and converting them into jobs?' He figured he made about $4,000 a week doing that.

"Then I said 'Fred, do the math.' Needless to say, he went right out and hired someone to do the running around, and he took that extra 15 hours to focus on selling more roofing jobs. That one strategy helped take him from a $300,000-per-year business which was heavily laden in debt to the IRS, to a $3.5-million business with a 20 percent net profit margin and all of his IRS debts paid off."

"So, stop doing all these small jobs that I should be paying someone else to do?" Eric asked rhetorically as he glanced wistfully out into the repair bays.

"That's right," Mike said. "If we look at all the tasks that you do, most of them could be done at a fraction of the price that you should be paying yourself."

"Ok," Eric said, "but that still doesn't address the point that in the past I have allowed others to do these tasks, and they have failed miserably costing me untold thousands. What you're asking me is to repeat a process that hasn't worked in the past."

"It hasn't worked in the past because you didn't do it right," Mike said. "I bet you would give people instructions on tasks they were to do, and when they didn't do them correctly, you would just get mad and go do them yourself. Pretty soon, they figured they would just get out of your way and go find something else to do. Or they would goof around while you worked your tail off."

"That's exactly what's been going on," Eric replied angrily.

"So instead, what if you had given them written instructions on exactly what to do, showed them how to do it, followed up with them to make sure they were doing it right, and then if they were not doing it right, coached them until they were ?"

"Doesn't that take more time than just doing it yourself?" Eric asked.

"Initially, of course," Mike said. "But let's go back to the idea that time is a more valuable resource than money. If you invested some initial time in developing very basic written systems, training your team to use the system, and then making sure they followed the systems through coaching and follow up, that initial investment would pay off via reduced time on your part...time you would have spent doing all those things yourself."

"Ok, I guess now that you look at it that way, I am a control freak. I just never realized how this has hurt my business," Eric said looking around his office. "Since I've had no systems in place, I've learned to distrust my team members, thereby forcing me to keep tight control of virtually everything around here."

"I think we just had a breakthrough," Mike said with a great big smile. "Now let's take a look at the next step."

What should you be delegating today?
"Now it's time to figure out what you should start delegating

as soon as possible... maybe even today if that can be done," Mike said. "Now realize, Eric, that when you have a wounded business, you have to look at the first few things you can delegate. It makes no sense to delegate tasks at a pace faster than you can reasonably create a basic system, train your team, and then follow up with them. I've seen too many wounded business owners want to accelerate this process and thereby lose control of the tasks that they delegated out."

"I see all these tasks that I do from the study," Eric exclaimed, "but which ones do I delegate first?"

Mike reached over to his carefully organized stack of forms and pulled out a sheet of paper with four boxes on it, and showed it to Eric.

"Eric, this is a simple exercise to help you figure out exactly what you should delegate first. Yes, this may look simple, but a good friend and fellow business coach loves to tell me 'Simple is sophisticated.' Let's take a look."

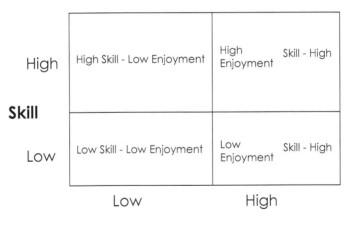

Low Skill-Low Enjoyment: Simple tasks you don't enjoy doing, such as sweeping floors.

Low Skill-High Enjoyment: Simple tasks you like to do, such as shopping for supplies at the store.

High Skill-Low Enjoyment: Tasks that demand a level of technical training and experience and you don't enjoy doing, such as filling out technical forms.

High Skill-High Enjoyment: Tasks that demand a level of technical training and experience and you enjoy doing, such as programming computers.

"What we want to do Eric is to take all of your tasks and put them in one of these four boxes. We then work at delegating out the low skill-low enjoyment tasks first. Once we have done that, we then work on delegating the low skill-high enjoyment tasks, then the high skill-low enjoyment tasks, and then finally the high skill-high enjoyment tasks. Does this make sense?"

"Yes, it does," Eric said, "but why would I delegate the low skill-high enjoyment tasks before the high skill-low enjoyment tasks? It seems to me you would want to keep doing what you like doing even if it's low skill."

"That's simple," Mike answered. "It's easier to systemize and delegate lower skill tasks to someone else. And remember, the name of the game is to get you constantly working at higher level skills."

"Got it," Eric responded.

"Ok, let's fill out one of these charts for you," Mike said as he pulled out a blank form for Eric to work with. Eric sat down and categorized his tasks into the four boxes.

"So it looks like I need to start handing over the bookkeeping duties and stop running deposits over to the bank. This is going to be tough for me since you know my history with bookkeepers and being embezzled," Eric said with some concern in his voice.

"Yes, I understand that," Mike answered. "That's why we need to address the next area of concern for unclogging your blocked artery of time."

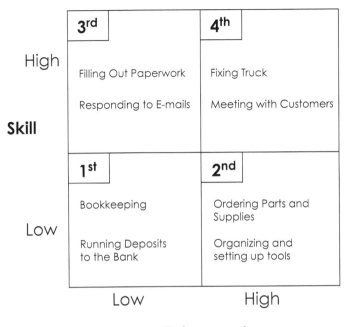

High	**3rd** Filling Out Paperwork Responding to E-mails	**4th** Fixing Truck Meeting with Customers
Low	**1st** Bookkeeping Running Deposits to the Bank	**2nd** Ordering Parts and Supplies Organizing and setting up tools
	Low	High

Skill (vertical axis)

Enjoyment

What should you not be delegating today?

"Now, I know I told you that a business is designed to be a commercial, profitable enterprise that should be able to work without you. This means that at some point in time, virtually 100 percent of any activity you would perform in your business will be delegated. However, since our focus at present is to stabilize your wounded business, let's look at some things that should not be delegated until well after the business is on its way to total health."

• Reviewing financial statements: Your job is to review your financial statements at least monthly. Look for trends that might indicate trouble and follow up on them to correct any actions. Corrupt bookkeepers look for business owners who don't know how or will not review their profit-and-loss statements, balance sheets, and statement of cash flows. This strategy along with your accountant will help you better understand what these statements mean, and how to spot trouble before it overtakes you.

• Final decisions on hiring employees: Although your

managers can source and interview candidates, you need to be the final authority on hiring people into your business. Until your business is stabilized, it's best that you conduct the final interview so that you know who is coming into your business. Poor hiring decisions are some of the worst decisions that can be made in a business.

•   <u>Problem solving with major clients and customers:</u> If there is a major problem with a customer who is vital to the success of your business, you need to be an important part of the solution. You cannot give this task over to someone else in your business without you personally having total awareness of what is going on and the solutions being discussed.

•   <u>Overall leadership of the organization:</u> Even if you are not a natural-born leader, it is still your responsibility to guide the direction of the business. The owner of a wounded business might want to give up total leadership of the organization in a desperate attempt to escape the pain of dealing with critical issues. While it is important to allow others within your business to make decisions and execute strategies, you, the business owner, must never forget that the bottom-line is it's still your business. Therefore, you must be the final decision maker for the most important decisions that occur in your business.

"Ok, I'm starting to get a lot clearer on this whole delegation process. I know I have a long road ahead of me, but I'm ready to start tackling my time issues," Eric mentioned as he went over the information with Mike.

"That's great." Mike said. "Now let's address another issue that I have noticed with you that is common among owners of wounded businesses."

Multi-Tasking is not a badge of honor.
"Eric, I notice that you like to multi-task. For example, I've seen you speaking with your team members while you were also checking e-mail, and looking at the caller ID when the phone rings. How is that working for you?"

"That is one I pride myself on," Eric beamed. "Once I actually conducted an entire conversation with a customer at the same time I was changing the head gasket on a truck, and eating a sandwich when my hands were free. Pretty impressive, huh?"

"Eric, you think you are being more productive when you multi-task, but actually the complete opposite is true. You are actually quite a bit less productive when you try to do multiple things at once. There was a study published in 2007 by Eric Horvitz, a Microsoft research scientist, and Shamsi Iqbal, from the University of Illinois, where they studied a group of Microsoft workers and found out that it took them, on average, 15 minutes to return to serious mental tasks, like writing reports or computer code, after responding to incoming e-mail or instant messages. They also tended to stray off to reply to other messages or browse news, sports or entertainment Web sites. (New York Times, March 25th, 2007) This supports multiple other studies showing that multi-tasking is not a productivity enhancer."

"Yeah, but my soon-to-be ex-wife used to be a secretary in an emergency room, and she kept telling me that you had to be a multi-tasker in order to be successful, so I'm sure you've had to do lots of multi-tasking in your time," Eric said with indignation.

"Eric, you are comparing apples to oranges," Mike shot back. "When I was in a trauma, I had multiple processes going on all at once, so it might have looked like I was multi-tasking. But in reality, I was focused on one thing, and one thing only, and that was saving the life of the patient. Let me give you a real-life business example. I had a client once who at my first initial meeting with him, kept obsessively kept checking and replying to his e-mails, even as he attempted to work with me on his business. Take a wild guess what he said was his number-one problem in his business."

"Not enough time?" Eric replied sheepishly.

"That's right. He was never focused on the most important things in his business because he was constantly multi-tasking, and therefore performing all of his multiple tasks poorly."

"So what do you suggest that I do?" Eric asked

"Break down major tasks into blocks of two hours each," Mike said. "Within the block, work on that one thing and one thing only. Close your door or hit the do-not-disturb button on your phone to make sure you don't get distracted. Once you are finished with that task, come out of your office, take 20 minutes to walk around, deal with any issues as necessary, and then go back and work on another task for two hours. If you have tasks that take less than two hours, group similar tasks together in one two-hour block. The key here is to operate using focused activity, followed by a break before going back into another activity."

"Ok, that sounds great in theory, but I have employees who need access to me constantly, so I just don't see how this can work for me," Eric said as he shook his head.

"And this goes right back to your control freak nature," Mike said quickly. "You have trained your team to constantly interrupt you, so now it's time to retrain them not to rely on your attention for up to two hours at a time. I can assure you that the business will still be there when you come out of your office. It's time for your team to put on their big boy pants and learn to live without you."

"Ok, you win again," Eric said as he faked a disappointed expression and rocked back in his chair. "So where do we go from here?"

Putting your time plan together

"The most important thing I want you to do is to put together a default calendar," Mike said as he pulled another sheet of paper from his briefcase.

"What is a default calendar?" Eric asked as he looked at the sheet of paper.

"A default calendar is simply a time plan that you put together to lay out exactly how you plan to use time in your day. You start out by scheduling the most important tasks in your calendar first. Tasks such as business planning, employee development, and proactive marketing should be the highest priority. After that, you then insert time space for other tasks that need to happen on a daily basis. See the sample of one of my clients' default calendar on previous page.

"This makes sense, but why does he have 'time with Marcus' and 'exercise' listed in here?" Eric asked. "These don't look like business tasks."

Jason's Schedule Template

	Monday	Tuesday	Wednesday	Thursday	Friday	Saturday	Sunday
5:00	Wake up	Wake up	Wake up	Wake up	Wake up		
6:00	Exercise	Exercise	Exercise	Exercise	Exercise	Wake up	Wake up
7:00	Leave For Work	Leave For Work	Leave For Work	Leave For Work	Leave For Work		Exercise
	Daily Preview	Daily Preview	Daily Preview	Daily Preview	Daily Preview		
8:00	Business Building	Business Building	Business Building	Business Building	Business Building	Exercise	
9:00		Phone Calls					
10:00	Individual Staff Follow-ups	Appointment setting	Appointments & Phone Calls	Appointments & Phone Calls	Appointments & Phone Calls		
11:00		Proposal Follow-ups					
12:00	Lunch	Lunch	Lunch	Lunch	Lunch		Time with Marcus
1:00		Coaching with Dr. Mike					
2:00					Appointments & Phone Calls	Personal Time	
3:00	Appointments & Phone Calls		Appointments & Phone Calls	Appointments & Phone Calls	Weekly Staff Meeting		
4:00		Phone Calls					
5:00					Weekly Wrap Up	Time With Marcus	
							Personal Time
6:00	Daily Recap & Clean Up	Daily Recap & Clean Up	Daily Recap & Clean Up	Daily Recap & Clean Up	Daily Recap & Clean Up		
7:00	Personal Time	Personal Time	Personal Time	Personal Time	Personal Time		

"Jason's business was very similar to yours," Mike answered, "and like you, he went through a bad divorce where his wife finally gave up and left with their son, Marcus. One of his big issues was that he spent little or no time with Marcus after the divorce, and it was eating him up. We quickly identified this as one of his 'Big Rocks,' as Stephen Covey describes important tasks, which can sometimes be easily ignored by the busyness of business and life. I got him to schedule regular time with his son, and then held him accountable to make sure he actually carried through with what was on his calendar. It wasn't easy, and sometimes, I had to get on him for failing to spend time with Marcus. In the end though, he was able to stick to the default calendar, and he was able to turn his business around and rekindle his relationship with his son. In addition, he was suffering from health challenges due to his lack of exercise, so we put in daily exercise time. It made a huge difference in his life."

"This is really hitting to close to home," Eric said as he looked at pictures of his kids on the credenza beside his desk. "My wife and I get into constant fights about me not going to kids' events, or blowing off my weekends with them because I have to be here in the shop. I have to get this under control."

"Excellent, I'm glad that you're going to tackle this," Mike said. "However, once you have developed your default calendar, you have to discipline yourself to follow the calendar. It makes absolutely no sense whatsoever to put the time into developing this if you just ignore it. So we're going to use a simple measurement system to help you track how successful you are with following your plan. Let's take a look at how this works.

TIME OF DAY	Monday	Tuesday	Wednesday	Thursday	Friday
6:00AM					
6:30AM					
7:00AM					
7:30AM	Plan day	Plan day	Check email	Meeting with Jon	Meeting with Jon
8:00 AM	Check email	Meeting with Jon	Meeting with Jon	Homework stuff	
8:30 AM	Meeting with Jon	Sales calls		Update website	
9:00 AM	Sales calls	Sales calls	Sales calls	Update website	
9:30 AM	Sales calls	Sales calls	Meet with customers in shop	Update website	
10:00 AM	Sales calls	Check on shop projects	Sales calls	Invoicing	
10:30 AM	Sales calls		Homework		
11:00 AM	Sales calls		Meeting with equipment salesman		
11:30 AM	Sales calls		Meeting with equipment salesman		
12:00 PM	Lunch	Lunch	Lunch		Travel to Portland
12:30 PM	Lunch	Lunch	Lunch	Lunch	Travel to Portland
1:00 PM	Check email	Sales meetings	Proposals	Lunch	Travel to Portland
1:30 PM	Meeting with customer	Proposals	Proposals		Travel to Portland
2:00 PM	Meeting with customer	Proposals			Travel to Portland
2:30 PM	Payroll	Proposals	Sales calls		Travel to Portland
3:00 PM	Proposals	Proposals	Sales calls		Travel to Portland
3:30 PM	Proposals	Sales calls	Sales calls		Travel to Portland
4:00 PM	Sales calls	Call vendors	Research shop equipment		Travel to Portland
4:30 PM	Research products	Research shop equipment	Research shop equipment		Travel to Portland
5:00 PM		End day	End day		Travel to Portland
5:30 PM	End day				Travel to Portland

"Once you've developed your default calendar, then you track your time on a daily basis and color code each block of time depending on what happened."

Dark Gray: You did what was on your default calendar.

Darkest Gray: You did not do what was on your default calendar.

Light Gray: You lost track of time, and do not recall if you stuck to your default calendar.

Medium Gray: Fixed appointments that were going to happen no matter what.

"In this example, the individual was supposed to work on payroll from 2:30 to 3 p.m. on Monday, but did not do that. However, this individual did work on proposals, sales calls, and research products from 3 to 5 p.m. on Monday. Very quickly, you will be able to see how successful you are at following your default calendar. Typically, when I get a business owner to follow this system, they can go from up to 70 percent darkest gray and light gray to 75 to 80 percent dark gray in six to eight weeks."

"Wow, this is going to take some serious discipline," Eric said as he looked at the default calendar and color-coded tracking system. "But I guess at this point there is no turning back."

"Ok, so let's recap what you will work on to unclog your blocked artery of time," Mike said as he grabbed Eric's case file and began to take notes.

Eric began to list them out:

1. Find out where I am wasting my time.
2. Stop my control-freak tendencies.
3. Put together a delegation plan.
4. Stop multi-tasking.
5. Identify my "Big Rocks" in my business and my life.
6. Put together a default calendar.
7. Implement a time-measurement system to track my success in following my default calendar.

"You know what the very first thing I am going to do to tackle this issue?" Eric said as he looked at Mike and smiled.

"No, what?" Mike replied

"I'm going to call my kids, and tell them to get ready for this Saturday. We are going to go to the park and spend some time swimming in the river, playing at the playground, and just having an all-around great time. And then we're going to go back to my house and barbeque hamburgers and hot dogs."

"I love it," Mike said with a big grin on his face. "Take some photos and send them over to me."

Now it's your turn. List all of the things that you need to do in your business to unclog your blocked artery of time. Your business may be different than Eric's truck-repair company, so your challenges will be unique to you. Put down what you will do, when you will do it, and who will help you accomplish the task.

Task	By When	Who Will help you
1.		
2.		
3.		
4.		
5.		
6.		
7.		
8.		
9.		
10.		

Chapter

5

*Pain- Getting Your
Customers To Love You...
Not Just Like You*

Rain pelted the steel roof of Clearwater Truck Maintenance and Repair as Mike walked in to face the challenges of another Tuesday. Soaking wet from the torrential downpour, Mike took off his overcoat and let the water drip onto the shop floor before going into the office area. He was excited to work with Eric on the next challenge, as they had been productive in previous weeks in getting Eric's time constraints under control. Mike was especially happy that Eric actually took a Friday afternoon off to go see his kids' soccer games. As a way of saying congratulations, Mike bought him a genuine World Cup soccer ball with Landon Donovan's personal signature to give to Eric's son, Josh, who had a life-size poster of Landon in his room.

"Is that what I think that is?" Eric asked as he saw the ball in the box that Mike was carrying.

"I hope Josh likes it. I cashed in on a big favor an old client owed me. It took a few phone calls, but we got the signature on the ball from the player himself," Mike said with an obvious sense of satisfaction.

"Josh told me the other day that his dream in life is to score the winning goal in the World Cup and hoist the trophy for the entire world to see," Eric said with immense pride. "And you know what? I believe he'll do it. He is going to be so happy to see this soccer ball."

"I'm sure he will," Mike said. "So let's get down to business. How are we doing at winning the game of business?"

"Well, it seemed to be getting better until a few days ago, and then I got the bomb dropped on me yesterday."

"What bomb?" Mike asked

"We have been losing more than our regular share of clients over the past few months, and I just figured that was just a normal part of business as some of our clients try out cheaper truck repair shops. However, I got a phone call from our biggest customer, Pendleton Trucking. They account for about 20 percent of our business. The President of the company, Jim, who has been a good friend of mine for years, told me that they have decided to pull all of their business away from us and give it to my main competitor. I don't know if I'm going to survive this," Eric said with an obvious tone of anxiety in his voice.

"Did he say why he is leaving you?" Mike asked

"Yeah, and where do I start?" Eric said in disgust. "He said that our deliveries are almost always late, the repairs are botched half the time. Our staff is rude and defensive when mistakes are brought up, and our billing is full of mistakes. It just pisses me off that he would take our mistakes so personally. Who does he think we are?" Eric said as he flung a file across the room and into a chair. Paper flew everywhere as it hit with the full force of Eric's wrath.

"He thinks you are a business that should be able to do a lot better than you are right now," Mike said in his normal, calm voice.

"What?" Eric said raising the volume of his voice. "He should be grateful with how many times we have bailed him out due to his driver's incompetence."

"No, you should be grateful he was honest with you," Mike said as he lowered his voice in an attempt to calm Eric down. "Eric, it's time to deal with pain in your body."

"I'm assuming you mean my business body," Eric said knowing where this was going, and not really willing to face the truth just yet.

"Yes, that's right," Mike said sensing that Eric was resisting a teachable moment. "Let me ask you this. When you get a pain in a part of your body, where does that pain come from?"

"Well I know that when my back hurts, it's usually because my spine is out and I need an adjustment from my chiropractor," Eric said.

"That's right. The pain in your back is merely a reflection of the problem that you are having with your physical body, namely your spine. And guess what?" Mike said.

"Let me guess, my customer problems are the pain that my

business body originates from my own issues," Eric answers as he slowly comes to the realization that maybe, just maybe, Mike is right.

"You got it," Mike answers with a hint of satisfaction. "Losing customers is just the pain symptom that emanates from the internal issues that you have inside of your business. When you lose good, long-term customers, the real reason lies in your failure to execute the basics of delivering your services to your customer."

"Ok, it's official, now I'm hurting," Eric said. "What needs to happen to get my customers happy again?"

"Let's take a look at this."

Do your customers even like you in the first place?

"The first thing we have to look at is the fact that your customers may have gotten tired of you and have left you without even telling you," Mike said.

"I'm confused by the statement," Eric interjected. "I've been friends with a large portion of my customers for years, and we talk about everything."

"Including the problems that they have with how you deliver your repair services?"

"Well, sometimes," Eric answered, wondering where this was going.

"I'm sure you have noticed some of your customers trucks haven't been in for repairs in a long time," Mike said. "Do you think that is because they have bought brand-new trucks and don't need your repair services?"

"Heck no," Eric answered. "Many of them are just as tight on finances as I am, so there is no way they are able to replace their trucks. Besides, if they did, the trucking community is pretty tight and we would see or hear about those new trucks."

"So, where did they go?" Mike asked. "Did they tell you that they weren't going to have their trucks repaired in your facility?"

"I don't know," Eric answered feeling a bit ashamed. "I would have hoped they would have said something to me."

"Let's say you have a favorite restaurant, and you know the owner real well. After a few bad meals, you decide you don't want to eat there anymore. Are you going to seek him out and tell him why you won't eat there anymore?"

"Well, no," Eric answered slowly. "I just wouldn't want to offend him, and besides, I'm not real good with conflict, so I guess it's just easier not to go there anymore."

"Do you think that might be happening with some of your customers?" Mike asked, making his point.

"Ok, now I see that it's just easier for them not to say anything to me," Eric answered. "I wondered why they were never available when I tried to call."

"You see, when your customer has had a bad experience with your business, they generally won't tell you, but the sad thing is that they will tell others. According to RightNow Technologies 2009 Customer Experience Report, consumers are taking their anger and acting on it via word of mouth and social channels. This report shows that 82 percent of consumers that had a bad experience told others about it, up 22 percent since 2006. Many consumers that had a bad experience and told others about it shared their experience online by posting a negative customer review on the company's Website (23 percent), Facebook (7 percent), or a blog (6 percent). More and more customers are telling everybody they know about bad experiences, everybody except, in some cases, the company that gave the bad service. Go online and type in 'bad customer service experiences" in Google. You get untold thousands of hits."

"Ok, so what do I need to do to get customers to start loving me again?" Eric asked.

Survey your customers

"The first thing we need to do is to determine what your customers are thinking about you right now, so we need to do a survey of your customer base and get their opinions."

"Why do we need to jump through those kinds of hoops?" Eric asked. "If I know my customers don't like me, why spend time, energy and money to formalize what's already obvious?"

"Because you may think you know why your customers don't like you, but the real reason they don't like you may be something completely different. Let me tell you a story. Once I was working with a dental lab whose sales started dropping off. It was obvious that the dentists were sending their work somewhere else, so the owner was convinced that it was a quality issue with their work. He had been focusing on refining their quality. Nevertheless, they kept losing customers. I had him survey his customers, and he was shocked by the results."

"What were they?" Eric asked

"The customer's number-one problem was a complete lack of on-time delivery. The lab had been so obsessed with quality that they were sending the orders out late in order to get the products absolutely perfect. In the meantime, the dental offices were getting more and more upset because their patients were not being delivered what they had been promised. So, they found other labs that could deliver products on-time even if the quality level was not as good as what my client produced."

"Wow, interesting story," Eric exclaimed. "I wonder if I perceive my customer's problems with my company the wrong way... sort of like that lab."

"That could very well be the case, but we won't know it until we ask the customers, so let's get started," Mike said.

"I'm not sure where to begin," Eric said

"Let's pretend that we are a customer and that we are doing business with you. What are all the steps that a customer would go through in their experience with you? I also call these, 'The Moments of Truth,' times when it's necessary to impress your customer with your service."

"Hmmm, let's see. I guess it would start with the initial phone call to schedule a repair. After that, the moments of truth would be: when they come in and drop off the truck, how fast we fixed the truck, how clean our facility was, whether we explain adequately what repairs were done, whether our staff was friendly, the quality of the repair work, and whether the invoice was easy to read."

"Excellent," Mike said. "Now let's break these steps down and put them on a scale of 1-5 for the customer to rate. Here is an example of the start of what a survey form might look like:

Please rate the quality of your experience with Clearwater Truck Maintenance and Repair by answer the following Questions on a scale from 1 to 5, with one being the lowest and 5 being the highest:

(Circle the most appropriate response to the following questions)

The initial contact with the Clearwater team

Poor	Below Average	Average	Above Average	Excellent
1	2	3	4	5

Efficiency in dropping off the truck

Poor	Below Average	Average	Above Average	Excellent
1	2	3	4	5

Speed of repair

Poor	Below Average	Average	Above Average	Excellent
1	2	3	4	5

Cleanliness of Clearwater facility

Poor	Below Average	Average	Above Average	Excellent
1	2	3	4	5

Clarity of what repairs were done

Poor	Below Average	Average	Above Average	Excellent
1	2	3	4	5

Friendliness and responsiveness of Clearwater team members

Poor	Below Average	Average	Above Average	Excellent
1	2	3	4	5

Effectiveness of repair

Poor	Below Average	Average	Above Average	Excellent
1	2	3	4	5

Invoice correct and understandable

Poor	Below Average	Average	Above Average	Excellent
1	2	3	4	5

Overall rating of your experience with Clearwater

Poor	Below Average	Average	Above Average	Excellent
1	2	3	4	5

Additional Comments:

"Ok, so I see how you broke down all the touch points that a customer might go through and have a quantifiable rating for each so I could see where our customer perceived we were dropping the ball," Eric said as he looked at the form.

"That's correct," Mike said waiving his pen over the form. "Now I know that this is simply a draft and that you may come up with some revisions and additions to cover as many of the customer experience points as possible, but you got the idea, right?"

"Yeah, I got the idea. However, how do I get this into my customer's hands?"

"Good question," Mike said. "Up until a few years ago, you either had to mail out survey forms hoping your customers would fill them out and sent them back, or you'd have to make telemarketing calls to ask the questions, or survey them when they are on-site. However, today the Internet makes this process oh-so simple. There are several simple services where you can send an e-mail out to your clients with a link that they can click on and in a few short minutes complete the form. Very simple, very easy."

"Hmmm, my customers don't work well with technology," Eric mused as he looked at the questionnaire. "Most of them are pen-and-paper kind of guys."

"Maybe, but my experience is that if you use the old-fashioned method of mailing them out, you may get 4 or 5 responses out of 100. You're asking people to open an envelope, pull out a pen, write down their responses, stuff the survey back in an envelope, and then actually carry the envelope all the way to the mail box. That's a lot of work and somebody may break a sweat doing it," Mike said as Eric chuckled. "When you send the survey electronically, all a person has to do is open an e-mail, click on the link in the e-mail, click on their survey choices, maybe type in a few written responses, and click on the send button. When you use this method, you can typically get 15 to 20 responses out of 100, which, needless to say, is a much better sample size."

"What are some of the services out there that I can use?" Eric asked.

"My favorite is Survey Monkey (www.surveymonkey.com). It's very simple to develop the survey and upload the e-mails, and it's free for the first 100 response surveys you send out. There are some other services out there that you can also research."

"Once you find out what your customers think about you, now we need to take a look at the next step in relieving your pain in getting your customers to love you."

Start with consistency before you try for brilliance

"The next thing we need to look at is delivering your service with systematic consistency. Too many wounded businesses try to be brilliant with their service before they have the basics nailed down."

"So what do you mean by that?" Eric asked.

"Let me tell you a funny story from my youth," Mike said as he started moving his hands. "When I was 16, I had a big-time crush on a girl at my high school named Cindy. I would do just about anything to impress her. When I was skiing one day I was on a black diamond run, which is one of the most difficult runs on the mountain. I saw Cindy about 70 meters below me and I said to myself 'I'm going to go by her and show her what a brilliant skier I am.' I got going and was doing great. My form was perfect, and my technique was flawless. Right before I got to her, I made a mistake, tripped and fell, and tumbled head over heels right past her. She skied up to me and said 'Oh, hi Mike, it's you. Are you hurt?' 'No I'm fine,' I said as I picked myself up, brushed the snow off of me, and put my skis back on, along with my pride."

"That's a great story," Eric said as he laughed. "But what does that have to do with my business?"

"Your customer service is sort of like my skiing at 16, wanting to be brilliant and impressive, but falling down at the point of delivery, and your customer only sees your mess-ups."

"Isn't that the truth," Eric said as he shook his head. "We have extremely skilled mechanics with more certifications and experience than any other shop in a three-state region, but we constantly drop the ball. How is that happening?"

"Because you have trained your people to believe that the repair has to be brilliant, but nothing else matters. Let me ask you this Eric, does McDonald's make the best hamburgers in the world?"

"No"

"Do you care?"

"Not really," Eric responded.

"Eric, you care that the same hamburger you get in Kennewick is the same hamburger you get in New York, and it's the same hamburger you'll get in Berlin." Mike said, tossing his empty coffee cup into the trash. "Your customers care that your team members treat them well, that they are communicated with, that the repair is done in a timely fashion, and that the repair works. At their core, they don't care that you have used the newest part or the fanciest technique to get the job done, they just want their truck delivered at the day and time when you said you would."

"I'm getting the point," Eric muttered as he looked out into his repair bays. "I guess if we are brilliant one day, and lousy the next, what does our customer remember?"

"Lousy," Mike responded.

"So now what?" Eric asked looking for guidance.

"Let's go back to what we discussed about in the survey. I want you to put yourself in your customer's shoes and walk through the customer's experience of dealing with Clearwater Truck Maintenance and Repair. Look at each and every interaction that they would have with you, right from the first phone call all the way to driving the truck away after the repair and even beyond that. Where are you typically falling down? Find ways to tighten up those areas instead of just focusing on the repair itself. Your customer must get the feeling of consistency every time they visit you. They need to know what to expect when they deal with you instead of playing the lottery and 'hoping' for a brilliant experience."

"That's a great start," Eric said as he started to take notes. "However, I have a much bigger problem that needs to be solved before I move forward in this area."

"I know where you're going with this, but why don't you tell me in your own words," Mike said as he leaned back in his chair.

Getting your team to love your customers

"All I hear all day long from my team is how our customers are a bunch of idiots. They joke about supposed customer stupidity and say that customers ask for way too much. I even heard one of our technicians tell a customer over the phone, 'I don't have time for your problems right now, I have trucks to fix.'"

"Did you say something to that mechanic?" Mike asked.

"No, he's my best mechanic, and I'm afraid if I piss him off, he'll go to work for my competition."

"Have you ever told your team how much each customer is worth to your business?"

"No, why would that be important? My team doesn't need to know the financial details of this business," Eric said obviously getting defensive.

"That is where you are dead wrong," Mike said. "Let's say that conversation with your 'best mechanic' drove away your customer forever. How much does a typical customer spend with you a year?"

"Oh I don't know, probably about $5,000 per year," Eric said.

"And your gross profit is about 40 percent as we discussed several weeks ago, correct?"

"Yeah, that's about right," Eric replied.

"Let's say you plan on being in business another 20 years before you finally sell the business and go into a glorious retirement. That typical customer would spend $100,000 with you, and you would generate $40,000 in gross profit alone. Now, how do you think your mechanic would react if he knew that his flippant five-second remark could potentially cost the company $40,000?"

"I guess he would choose his words more wisely," Eric said as he thought about it some more.

"And $40,000 is being conservative. Add up all the lost referrals that customer would have given you, and then all the negative word-of-mouth that the customer would have generated, and it adds up to hundreds of thousands, and perhaps millions of dollars. Don't tell me your team doesn't need to know the dollar value of a customer."

"Ok, I think I just got my rear-end handed to me," Eric said, knowing he really stepped on it with Mike.

"One time, just to illustrate this concept with employees of one of my clients, I had them gather around a fire pit, and I handed each of them $10,000 in fake $100 dollar bills. I didn't tell them the bills were fake; I made the copies as real as possible without breaking the law, so at first, they thought they were holding real cash. I had each of them give an example of bad customer service, then had them toss the $10,000 into the pit. When I was finished, I sprayed lighter fluid on the stack of money and lit it on fire as I described what these actions meant to the company in real financial terms. It was a huge wake-up call for the team."

"Wow, what a way to make a point," Eric said

"So getting back to my point, Eric, your best performer doesn't belong in your company if he or she doesn't view the customer as the ultimate source of their paycheck. This may seem obvious to you and me, but it isn't to a typical employee as they get their paycheck no matter how profitable or unprofitable your business operates. You have to change your employees' mindsets so they see their interactions with customers as having a DIRECT impact on the company—and ultimately their job."

"Ok, this is good, but we find that the majority of our customers come across as demanding and pushy," Eric said. "They expect us to work miracles, and when we come through with the miracles, they don't even say thank you. They just drive away. What's with that?"

"That's because you have trained your customers to be pushy," Mike said as he leaned forward toward Eric. "Since you don't give them what they expect to get from you, many just leave your business, and the ones that stay learn that they have to be demanding, rude, and obnoxious in order to get any level of satisfaction. Let me give you another story. Years ago, there was a restaurant owner in Seattle who had a team member come up to him to ask him a question. One of the customers he was serving asked for a pickle on his sandwich that normally didn't come with a pickle. He asked the owner what he should do since this was out of the ordinary. Should he allow the customer to have the pickle? Should he charge the customer for a side of pickles? 'Oh for God's sake, just give him the pickle,' the owner admonished the server. That one concept spread through the entire team, and they started to find ways to make the customers delighted with the restaurant, and give the customers what they wanted, or as they said, 'Give them the pickle.' So let me ask you, Eric, what does your team need to do to give your customers the pickle?"

Eric sat there and thought for what seemed like an eternity. "I think we can start by addressing all of our customers by name when they come in here instead of 'Yeah, what do you want' like we usually do."

"That's a good start," Mike said. "There are probably several dozen ways that you can give your customers 'The Pickle,' but you have to start somewhere."

"Now I need to start putting something together so this all happens," Eric said. "Let's discuss how I'm going to do this."

Putting basic systems in place so you can easily love your customer

"The first thing we need to do is to map out the entire customer experience in your business and walk in their shoes as I discussed earlier," Mike said as he started taking notes. "At each key point in the process, we will need to script out the process of what you want to happen so that the customer has a great experience with you and your business. For example, what is the phone script you'll have your team use when the customer calls in to make a repair appointment? What is the process for diagnosing a problem with the vehicle and how will you effectively communicate the recommended fixes? How often will you communicate with the customer during the repair process, and what is the procedure for dealing with a customer who is not satisfied with your service?"

"That seems like a lot of work," Eric said thinking about the enormity of the task.

"Let's start with some basics that are going to help you solve up to 80 percent of your system challenges," Mike said. "One of the most important basics is getting your customer information into a working Customer Relationship Management system so we can start tracking who exactly are your customers. What do you use right now to keep track of your customers?"

"Paper records and filing cabinets," Eric said as he pointed over to a group of slightly rusting file cabinets with paper hanging out of some of the drawers.

"And how's that working for you?" Mike responded

"Not so good. I guess you are going to tell me it's time to get into the modern world," Eric said as his head started calculating the cost of new computer and software systems.

"That's right," Mike said as he took a piece of paper and threw it into the trash as a not-so-subtle way of telling Eric what needed to be done. "I know right now you are thinking that you can't afford to invest in any sort of technology, especially when it comes to customer service. I'm telling you that you can't afford not to invest. Let me ask you this, Eric, have you ever lost customers because you couldn't find old customer service records in a timely fashion and therefore couldn't help them as you would have liked?"

"I could tell you probably at least 10 former customers who got frustrated with our record keeping system and never returned again," Eric said as he shook his head

"So $40,000 lifetime value of your customer times ten equals at least $400,000. And you're telling me you can't afford a Customer Relationship Management (CRM) system?" Mike said with a touch of irony in his voice.

"Why are you always right?" Eric said with a smirk on his face.

"Because you're not the first business who has had these problems and you won't be the last," Mike said as he finished taking his notes.

"So, do I need to go out and get a fancy new CRM system right now?" Eric asked.

"You will eventually need to do that," Mike said. "But for now, even if you just develop some Excel spreadsheets with your customer's basic information, that is at least a start. Let's start off with simple and work our way up the ladder."

"Makes sense to me," Eric said, relieved that he wasn't going to have to fork over loads of cash right away.

"There is one more thing we need to cover to start getting your customers to love you and not just like you, and it's probably the most important thing we will cover today," Mike said.

"What's that?" Eric asked.

On-going communication: the painkiller for the pain of dealing with your customers.

"It's time we start looking at how you will communicate with your customers on a regular basis," Mike said as he flipped through some notes. "How do you do that right now?"

"Basically we don't," Eric said. "The only time they hear from us is when we send them invoices and statements."

'Gimme your money' is the only message you give to them after they have worked with you," Mike said. "Rather impersonal, isn't it?"

"I never thought of that way," Eric said

"Suppose you were married, and all you did night after night was come home and ask, 'Where's my dinner?' without saying anything else to your wife. How long do you think that marriage would last?"

"To be honest, that is basically what happened with my marriage," Eric said as he looked at the picture of his soon-to-be ex-wife whose photo still graced his desk. "I would come home after a long, hard day of work, and all she would want to do is talk. I just wanted dinner and a little peace and quiet. After awhile, she stopped talking to me, and then one day she served me divorce papers along with my supper. Yeah, there were a lot of other things going on, but at the core, I quit communicating with her and after awhile, she stopped trying."

"And that's exactly what's happened between you and all of your valuable customers. Since you never communicated with them beyond 'Where's my dinner?' basically what you were telling them when you sent out your invoices and statements was that you didn't really care about them. So of course they were going to divorce you."

"Ok, so on-going communication with my customers is the antidote when my customer service fails," Eric said, as he began to grasp the concept.

"You got it," Mike said, excited that Eric was catching on quickly. "Think about the old-style balancing scales. On one side of the scales you have deposits and on the other side of the scale you have withdrawals. In a business relationship, withdrawals happen when you do not meet your customer's expectations. Perhaps you're late in getting a repair done, or maybe you incorrectly billed out items that shouldn't have been there. I don't care how great a business you are, withdrawals are going to happen. Deposits are when you meet and exceed customer expectations, such as delivering a repair early, or finding a hidden problem that allows your customer's trucks to run even better than before. If your deposits continue to be more than your withdrawals, then you will keep the customer. When withdrawals start to become more than your deposits, you will still keep the customer for a period of time until your deposits go to zero. That's when your customer leaves you."

"So, what you're saying is having an on-going communication system is like continually putting deposits onto the scale that can be used to overcome any withdrawals," Eric said.

"That's it," Mike said. "Let's talk about where we start."

"A newsletter?" Eric asked

"Not yet," Mike said. "Let's go back to your 'Where's my din-ner' form of communication called invoices and statements. What could you include in your statements that would positively commu-nicate with your customers?"

"I could certainly put in a coupon for a free lube, oil and filter with any repair over $300," Eric said. "Or I could put in some mainte-nance alerts from the main-truck manufactures, or perhaps even something personal about one of the team members."

"Excellent," Mike exclaimed. "You will get your dinner without demanding it, and at the same time, they'll be appreciative of the fact you've done the equivalent of asking what you can to help around the house."

"Yeah, I would have saved my marriage had I done that," Eric said as he continued to look at his ex-wife's picture on his desk. "You know, I've never been a real good communicator in my life, and I guess it's shown up in both my marriage and my business."

"But Eric, it's never too late to start a new habit," Mike re-minded him. "Once you get your Customer Relationship Manage-ment system up to speed, you can start keeping track of significant events in your customers' lives such as birthdays, anniversaries, and their children's birthdays."

"And why is that important?" Eric asked.

"Have you ever received an unexpected card in the mail?" Mike asked.

"Yes."

"How did it make you feel?"

"It made me feel like someone cared," he paused. "Ok, now I see where you're going with this."

"Remember this, Eric, at the end of the day, it's not what you say or what you do, but how you make people feel that matters the most. When you send birthday cards to your customers or send them a personal thank-you note for doing business with you, you are making them feel like you truly care about them, which I know you do."

"So the emotional connection is what I'm really aiming for in my communication with my customers," Eric responded.

"You got it."

"So how does a newsletter come into play with this whole communication strategy?" Eric asked.

"Your newsletter is your vehicle to let your customers take a look at what's going on deep inside the bowels of Clearwater Truck Maintenance and Repair," Mike responded. "They get to meet the real 'Eric' and find out interesting things that they may have never known about you or your team."

"And what would I put into a newsletter?"

"Anything that will be of interest to them. Remember, you are writing it so they will get to know you better and be more interested in you at the same time. Maybe you could write an article on your thoughts about the state of the trucking industry, maybe put in a team-member profile, or even ideas to solve emergency problems when you can't be there. Heck, you might even put a favorite recipe in there. I had my pool maintenance retailer send me a newsletter with a wonderful kebab recipe. I cooked it up at my barbeque, and it turned out great. There are some great resources out there for writing an excellent newsletter."

"Do I send it electronically or by mail?" Eric asked. "I know mailing them out is going to be mighty expensive, but I know that I like a paper copy vs. e-mail. However, there are some pretty nice e-mail newsletter systems I've heard of, and it would be a lot cheaper. I'm afraid they will just get deleted before they are ever opened. What are your thoughts, Mike?"

"At this point, there really is not one right or wrong answer,"

Mike said. "Yes, you will certainly get a better response if you create a paper version and send it out in the mail, but you are right, it will be much more difficult to develop if you do it yourself. It will be much more expensive if you have someone else do it, and there are the mailing and printing costs. If you're going to send e-mail newsletters, I would recommend you use a service instead of doing it yourself. The best known one out there is Constant Contact (www.constant-contact.com). It's inexpensive and extremely easy to use. Another service I would recommend is using STORM (Simple, Track-able, Organized, Repeatable Marketing) from Rainmaker Marketing (www.spokanerainmaker.com). It will definitely be more expensive than Constant Contact, but its templates will look much nicer, and you will have a much deeper and easier way to track how well your e-mails are being opened and utilized by your customers."

"Well, it looks like I have a lot of work to do to get my customers back to loving me again," Eric said as he looked down at his notes. "However, I guess there is no better time to start than now."

"Ok, so let's recap what you will work on to eliminate your customer pain points and get them to start not only loving you, but doing business with you again," Mike said as he grabbed Eric's case file and began to take notes.

Eric began to list them out:

1. Send out a survey to all my customers.
2. Identify all our customer interaction points and script out as much as possible.
3. Start giving our customers our version of "The Pickle."
4. Begin the process of developing and/or selecting a Customer Relationship Management System.
5. Put a special offer in our invoice and mailing state ments.
6. Send out personal cards to customers.
7. Begin the development of a newsletter.

Now it's your turn. List all of the things that you need to do in your business to get your customers to love you and not just like you. Your business may be different than Eric's truck-repair business, so your challenges will be unique to you. Put down what you will do,

Task	By When	Who Will help you
1.		
2.		
3.		
4.		
5.		
6.		
7.		
8.		
9.		
10.		
11.		
12.		
13.		
14.		
15.		
16.		
17.		
18.		
19.		
20.		

Chapter

6

*Ambulance Ride
Do You Really Know
Where You're Going?*

The winter snows had finally arrived in Kennewick as Mike drove into the parking lot of Clearwater Truck Maintenance and Repair at 8 a.m. on a cold Tuesday morning. Mike's car fishtailed as he drove up the driveway; the trucks that had arrived earlier in the morning compacted the fresh snow into an icy mixture that made driving much more difficult. As Mike approached, he noticed that the lot seemed busier than usual, and there was a definite buzz of activity going on in the shop the likes of which he had not seen before. It had been a number of weeks since his last visit, and with each coaching session since then, Eric became more and more confident about the potential success of his business. Total sales were up, customers were coming back, and although they were still not where they wanted to be financially, at least now the company was breaking even and was cash flow positive. However, after his last coaching call, Mike could detect that Eric was starting to lose energy and enthusiasm. He started not following through on activities he needed to do, and the focus just didn't seem to be there. Mike knew he had a lot of work ahead of him today as he trudged through the snow-covered parking lot into the warm, heated offices of the business.

"Good morning, Eric," Mike said enthusiastically as he took off his jacket and hung it up on the coat rack in Eric's office.

"Good morning, Mike," Eric said less enthusiastically as he looked at some papers on his desk and sipped his morning cup of coffee.

"You must be excited to see the first snowfall of the winter. More broken axles to be fixed and more body work to repair with all the new fender benders coming your way," Mike said as he looked out into the busy shop bays and began to put on what looked like an Ambulance Technicians jacket.

"Yea, I should be excited, but I'm not," Eric said with a downcast look on his face.

"Why not?" Mike said, pretending to be surprised. "Your customer counts are up. Your personal hours that you're working in this business are starting to come down. You're actually making money. What is there to not be excited about?"

"Mike, I've been in this business now for going on 15 years, and I just don't know if I want to do this any longer. I don't know why it all of a sudden hit me, but I'm just not having any more fun doing what I'm doing. I just don't know how to get that fun feeling back."

"Well Eric, it looks like it's time for your ambulance ride to the emergency room," Mike said as he pulled out his stethoscope.

"What the heck are you talking about? I feel fine?" Eric said as he wondered to himself what his coach was talking about and why on earth he was carrying a stethoscope.

"I mean the ambulance ride for your business," Mike said as he then pulled out a very large injection needle and a bottle of what looked like a clear liquid that was meant to go into the needle.

"Uh, Mike, I don't do needles very well," Eric stammered as Mike drew the clear liquid into the injector. "Where are we going with this?"

"You'll see," Mike said with a slight grin as he squirted out the excess liquid until he had just the right amount left in the syringe. "But before we use what's in this needle, the first thing we'll need to do is to see if the ambulance ride is even necessary, or if we go straight to the morgue."

"What do you mean by that?" Eric asked, becoming more and more puzzled.

Is your burnout curable, or has it advanced too far?

"You see, over the past number of months, we have been working on stabilizing your business, just as paramedics would stabilize a patient out in the field. They look at the ABC's of Airway, Breathing, and Circulation to ensure that the patient can survive the ambulance ride into the emergency room. We've been practicing our own ABC's of Money, Time, and Customer Service Delivery. However, if there is a DNR on the patient, we can't do anything about the patient. We'll have to let him die.

"What is a DNR?" Eric asked.

"Do Not Resuscitate," Mike answered. "This is used when somebody has a terminal condition such as cancer and prolonging their life would only cause them more suffering and pain."

"So are you suggesting I have cancer?" Eric asked as he furrowed his brow and looked even more confused than a few minutes ago.

"Yes, you probably have business cancer, which is what I call burnout," Mike said as he twirled the stethoscope in his hands.

"You know what, now that you say it, I really am starting to feel burned out almost every day that I am here," Eric said as he shook his head. "There have been some days recently that I have questioned why I am even putting all the efforts, money, and energy into getting this business back up to speed."

"What we need to do now is to determine if your burnout cancer has spread too far and call you a DNR, or if we can stop the cancer and get you out of burnout," Mike said

"And how are we going to determine that?" Eric asked.

"Not we. YOU," Mike said with emphasis on the last word.

"Ok, so how am 'I' going to determine this?" Eric asked with renewed interest.

"You are going to answer one question that will lead you down that path."

"And what is that one question?"

"What makes me happy?"

"What makes me happy how?" Eric asked not quite understanding where this was going.

"When you look back on your life, and you look forward into

the future of your life, what are the activities, things, thoughts, events, decisions, and so forth that have brought you the most happiness?"

"Ok, wow...now that's a deep question. I've never really thought about what makes me happy. I guess I've spent most of my life just doing what I thought I should be doing."

"You see, Eric, the answer to this question will determine whether you should stick around and grow your company or find a way to sell this place. If you find out that what makes you truly happy is totally incongruent to what you are doing here, then no matter what you do here, in the end you will always have the same mediocre results and a mediocre life to go along with it. Is that what you really want?"

"No. Not at all," Eric said. "But the only thing I've ever known in my life is truck repair, so what else is there in life?"

"Let me tell you about a good friend of mine," Mike said as he got comfortable in his chair. "Jim was a tax accountant specializing in international tax issues when I met him. He asked me to look at his resume as he had just left his previous job. I noticed something about him that stood out like a sore thumb."

"What was that?"

"Jim had worked for nine different accounting firms in 18 years. He kept quitting or getting fired. I asked him the same question I just asked you. Come to find out, music made him happy. He wrote songs, and he even had a rock and roll band when he was young. He was an incredibly creative and talented artist. I asked him why he got into accounting. He told me both of his parents were accountants and that "no respectable son of theirs was going to spend the rest of his life wasting his time on song writing and music." They insisted he get an accounting degree. Worst thing a parent could have ever done for their child.

"So what became of Jim?"

"Jim realized that he was not going to be able to change his vocation after all these years, but what he could choose was his environment, so he got a job as an international tax accountant at a software company specializing in music and art media. The place oozes creativity. He is still there today and loving it."

"So I guess it's time to figure out what makes me happy," Eric said.

Eric and Mike spent the next several hours digging deep into Eric's past, looking at his passions and helping him figure out the why in his life. When the discussion was finally over, they both agreed that Clearwater really and truly was Eric's passion, and he needed to go to the next level in exploring what should be done to cure his ailing business.

"Ok now that I think I have that clear, what's next?" Eric asked.

What does your future look like?

"What we need to do is have you develop a vision for your business. In other words, where are you going with Clearwater?"

"I've never been a really big fan of this whole 'envision your future' crap. I think it's just a waste of time, and I have better things to do during my workday. My motto comes straight from Larry the Cable Guy...Git er done."

"And you're going to take business advice from a stand-up comedian?" Mike asked in a slightly derisive tone. "You see, that has been one of your problems over the years. You have been so busy just surviving that you have never had an idea where you are going. Let's just say that you and I went out to my car right now and you hopped into the passenger seat. What would you probably ask me?"

"Where are we going?" Eric answered.

"Yes, and how would you feel if I told you, 'I don't know, but at least we're driving.'?"

"Probably not very good," Eric answered.

"That right," Mike said. "Or another way I might put this is, 'If you don't know where you are going, all the roads will take you there.'"

"Ok, so let's admit that I've never been into this fluffy stuff. I've always been a nuts and bolts kind of guy so this doesn't come easy to me. How do I get a start?"

"In the book 7 Habits of Highly Effective People, Steven Covey said, 'Begin with the end in mind.' In terms of your vision, what do you want your business to be like when it's finished? How big will it become? What will it be known for? How many locations will you have? How will your business impact the world? You can think of this in terms of building a house. You wouldn't just start digging a foundation, pouring concrete, throwing up 2x4s, and just kind of figure it out as you went along, would you?"

"Hey, I had a friend who basically tried that method, and never completed his house," Eric said. "Big waste of time and money."

"That's right," Mike said. "That's why you develop a blueprint of what you want your house to look like before it's finished. Unfortunately, most businesses I encounter just kind of make it up as they go along. If you know what you want your business to look like when it's finished, then every decision you make and every activity you do is oriented towards achieving that ultimate pre-determined outcome."

"But what if I achieve my vision, and I don't like what I've built?" Eric asked.

"Have you ever remodeled a house?" Mike asked

"Yeah," Eric answered.

"Same principle. Your vision may change over time, but it's still vitally important to have that vision out there as a guide."

"Ok, I can see what a vision will do for me, but what about my employees? I know them and none of them deal well with all this fluffy stuff."

"Actually, the primary audience for a vision is not only you, but your employees as well," Mike explained as he approached a white board in Eric's office. "Your primary job as a leader is to enroll and inspire your team, and one of the main ways that you do it is to have a powerful vision statement that elicits emotion."

"I don't get it," Eric said as he watched Mike write on his white board. "My employees want a paycheck out of this place. That's what makes them happy."

"Eric, what is this a picture of?" Mike asked as he completed his drawing.

"Looks like a lemonade stand," Eric said.

"What percentage of kids do you think had a lemonade stand or some sort of money-making operation when they were little?" Mike asked.

"Probably just about 100 percent," Eric answered as he looked at the drawing.

"What percentage of adults do you think own a business in North America today?"

"Just guessing, probably around 5 percent."

"You are just about right," Mike answered as he wrote the 5 percent figure on the board. "So what happened between every kid being an entrepreneur and adulthood today when 95 percent of them work for somebody else?"

"Not sure. Maybe they value something different as adults versus when they were kids?"

"You are on the right track. There are two main values competing here, opportunity and security. When we were kids, we valued opportunity over security, but when we became adults, we ended up valuing security over opportunity as we established obligations in life for ourselves. Deep down, each one of your employees still has that opportunity and drive that was there as a kid. Do you know how they live it today?"

"I don't know."

"They live it vicariously though you," Mike said as he wrote Clearwater over the lemonade stand drawing. "Eric, when you are successful, they see that they had a role to play in that success. It gets them excited to know that they're building something that goes beyond them. The problem is that when you have no vision, your employees don't know where you're going, so they bail out of the 'automobile' of your business rather than wander around aimlessly. Sure, they might say when they quit that they're going to work for someone else who can pay them more, or might be closer to where they live. But deep down inside, they leave you because they don't see a future in working for you."

"Ouch," Eric said as it dawned on him suddenly exactly what was happening with some of his employees.

"That's why you need to paint the picture of a bright future for them, so that they will know the sacrifices they make today will result in a wonderful tomorrow for everybody in the company. Apple is a great example of this. Steve Jobs put a vision out there years ago to his team of 'An Apple on every desk' and inspired his team to fulfill that goal. There isn't an Apple on every desk today, but that doesn't matter. That vision allowed his team to think outside of the computer box to develop iPods, iPads, iPhones, and so many other things that have allowed Apple to propel him towards that vision.

"And a lot of employees probably got rich," Eric said

"Yes, and do you think they are happy today knowing that they stuck it out through the lean years of Apple?"

"I would imagine so," Eric said as he kept staring at the drawing on the board. "So, once I develop my vision, what do I need to do next?"

What is the path to achieving that future?

"The next step is to develop your mission statement, which is the roadmap to achieving your vision. Let's go back to the example of hopping in the passenger seat of my car, and you ask me, 'Mike where are we going?' I say to you, 'We are going to Camas. Washington.' You say 'Great. How are we going to get there?' and I say 'I don't have a clue.' How are you going to feel?"

"Not very good, especially given the fact that I have no clue where Camas is," Eric chuckled.

"Across the river from Portland, Oregon and east several miles, but the point I'm making here is that your vision needs a direction in order for it to be accomplished."

"So is a mission statement a detailed plan?" Eric asked

"Actually, no. A mission statement is a short statement of who you are as a business, what business you are in, who your customers are, and what makes your business special."

"We know what business we're in, so why do we have to re-state it?" Eric asked.

"What business do you think you're in?" Mike asked

"The truck repair business," Eric answered.

"Really? I want you to think beyond just that. What is it that you truly provide your customers Eric that helps them with their lives?"

"I guess we provide them the peace of mind that comes with knowing that their trucks have been fixed the right way," Eric answered.

"There you go," Mike answered. "The mission statement is really designed to be read primarily by your customers, to let them know how you are going to take care of them. They want to know what you're all about when it comes to helping them."

"Let's take a stab at this and see what we come up with," Eric said as he pulled out a pad and pencil.

"Great idea," Mike answered as he erased the lemonade stand off the white board and prepared to take notes.

Eric and Mike worked for about an hour going back and forth, and finally this is what they came up with.

The Mission of Clearwater Truck Maintenance and Repair is to provide the highest level of maintenance and servicing to long-haul vehicles in our region. We are a specialized repair facility with highly trained technicians. We treat each truck that we service as if it were our own. Our customers see us not just as another maintenance facility, but instead as partners who contribute to their overall profitability through our highly systemized approach to maintenance and repair. This approach allows our customers to have the highest on-road time within their peer groups. We provide total peace of mind to every trucker who has their rig worked on by Clearwater technicians.

"Wow, I like that," Eric said. "Heck, if I owned a trucking company, I'd do business with Clearwater after reading that mission statement."

"See, your new roadmap tells customers where you are going, and gives them the incentive to hop in the automobile with you knowing you know how to get to the 'Camas, Washington' of their business.

"This is great, but I get a feeling I need more focus than just a vision and mission statement."

"That's right. Let's take a look at the next thing we need to work on."

Stop the survival mindset and start planning for the future

"Eric, now that we've looked at setting up your vision and mission, it's time for us to start looking at some basic business planning

---

processes. Don't worry. We're not talking complex here."

"Good, because I don't deal well with complex," Eric said, starting to feel better about things in general.

"The first thing I want you to do is go get the book Mastering the Rockefeller Habits by Verne Harnish. That is the main resource guide that works the best in helping a business like yours put together a simple, effective plan. His website is www.gazelles.com, and has lots of resources that you can use.

"Ok. That sounds great."

"One of the first things that you will need to do is to come up with a BHAG." Mike said as he wrote the initials on the whiteboard.

"What is a BHAG? Almost sounds like what I used to call my wife when she was riding my rear end about something or another."

"No, that's not it," Mike said as he started to laugh. "BHAG stands for Big, Hairy, Audacious Goal. Basically, what I want you to do is set a goal that you would want to achieve. It's probably totally impossible right now, but you know it could be done some day."

"Something like perhaps achieve 100 percent on-time delivery of trucks in a one year period?"

"Yes, that would be a perfect example," Mike exclaimed. "While that's impossible right now, it could be done, and it would definitely stretch you. If you actually achieved that BHAG, what would that do for your company?"

"We could achieve almost 100 percent market share in truck maintenance and repair throughout this entire region," Eric said with renewed excitement in his voice.

"There's the idea," Mike said. "That would also help you develop your brand promise, which is the most important thing that you would want to stand for in your customers' eyes. Your brand promise is just that, what you promise to deliver consistently to the marketplace."

"Ok, that sounds good."

"Then you will need to develop some three- to five-year targets and also some one-year goals. Next you will start breaking them down into 90-day goals and plans,"

"Why shift so frequently?" Eric asked. "Isn't that a little bit of overkill? Other business owners I've talked to strictly use annual business plans."

"Because you can't eat the elephant in one sitting," Mike responded. "For a typical human attention span, trying to work a one-year plan without dividing it up is just too daunting. My experience is that business owners who craft an annual plan can only stick to that plan for about 60 days before they lose interest and stop following it.

"Should I also chunk the 90-day plans down into weekly and even daily plans?" Eric asked.

"Yes, the more granular you make a plan, the better chance you have of executing it," Mike explained. "However, the key is making sure that your team follows along on the 90-day plan. Remember, you can't do this all by yourself. You have to delegate to others in your leadership team to make sure they're doing what needs to be done. This is where weekly and even daily meetings are so key…because it establishes a rhythm in your business where your team expects over time to be held accountable. They even look forward to getting 'atta-boys' from you and your leaders when they get things accomplished on the 90-day plan."

"Ok, that makes a whole lot of sense about business planning. It's something I have never done in this place," Eric said as he nodded his head. "But what are you going to do with that needle?" Eric said as he saw that the needle was still sitting right where Mike left it; it was obviously meant for something in Mike's session today.

How you can develop hope-ium to dull the pain of your current situation?

"Oh yeah, the needle," Mike said as he reached for it and approached Eric. "This is what I call hope-ium. It's the secret serum that will make you a far happier business owner than you are now. It's the last thing we need to do on your ambulance ride to the emergency room. Do you want some of this?" Mike asked as he reached for an alcohol swab to prepare Eric's arm for the injection.

"Are you out of your mind?" Eric snapped as he backed up towards the wall in his office. "I don't do drugs, and there is no way you are going to inject me with that, that hope-ium crap into my body."

"Preciously," Mike said with a big smile as he pointed the needle into the air, and pushed all the liquid out in a fine stream that arched its way over Eric's head and onto the floor next to the door, forming a small puddle that seeped out into the bay. "That's because the only hope-ium that really works is what you create in your mind."

"I don't get it, what was in that needle?" Eric said looking both relieved and perplexed at the same time.

"Just water," Mike said as he capped the needle and put it back into his briefcase. "I have so much fun scaring the crap out of clients with that exercise," he said as he took off his ambulance driver jacket and laid it over Eric's office chair.

"So what is hope-ium"? Eric asked

"Hope-ium is the drug of hope you put into your mind that keeps you going even when it doesn't look like you are going to make it," Mike said as finished putting his stethoscope back in his briefcase. "Let me ask you a question, Eric. What runs through your mind when you get bad news about your business"?

"To be honest, probably that I'm doomed and that my creditors will show up and force me to close my doors tomorrow."

"And you know what that is? It's fear, and it's the biggest killer of hope," Mike said as he slammed his briefcase shut with a loud thud. "So here's a good question, are you still in business?"

"Well, yeah," Eric said with a surprise look.

"So, everything you have feared for the past several years has not come to pass, yet you pursue this fear in your mind on a day-to-day basis. It takes away your hope for success, and takes away any sense of peace you have in you, doesn't it, Eric," Mike said with a passion that Eric hadn't seen in awhile.

"You're right," Eric said. "But I don't have control over those thoughts. They just rush in every time I get an unexpected bill or a customer says he won't be bringing his trucks to my facility again."

"Yes, you do have control," Mike said. "You have to actively inject hope-ium into your mind every time you feel that fear come over you."

"So how do I do that?" Eric

"The first and most important thing you have to do is to envision what you're thinking about," Mike said as he wrote the phrase on Eric's white board. "You have to start becoming aware of what goes through your mind on a minute-by-minute and even second-by-second basis. If you don't pay attention, any sort of negative thoughts will just take over and run amok in your life."

"Don't I know that," Eric said as he shook his head and looked at the white board.

"The second thing is, stop the negative thoughts as soon as they occur," Mike said as he wrote that phrase on the white board.
"As soon as that fear comes into your mind, you have to consciously say to yourself, 'Stop now. I don't accept that thought.' This is going to be very difficult at first because you have been accustomed to allowing thoughts to wander wherever they may go. However, the more you do it, the easier it will become."

"Hmmm, that's a lot to ask," Eric asked as he continued to stare at the white board.

"I know you can do it," Mike said as he prepared to write on the board again. The last thing is, speak the thoughts you want in your mind and even aloud for more reinforcement. You need to deliberately say to yourself what it is you want so as to counteract the negative thoughts that you've just stopped. It isn't enough just to stop the negative thoughts. They have to be replaced with the positive thoughts, and when you speak them out loud, your brain will begin to accept them much faster than if you had just thought them out. Yes, it will seem strange and perhaps difficult at first, but the more you do it, the easier it will become."

"So that is how you create hope-ium in yourself?" Eric asked.

"Yes it is," Mike said as he circled all three phrases on the white board. "Is it simple? You bet. Is it easy? Not at all. However, the more discipline you put into it, the better you will become at putting hope-ium into your mind."

"Hey, at least I don't need the needle to inject myself with hope-ium," Eric said with a laugh. "And you know what, if I do it long enough, I might even end up with a hope-ium addiction, which wouldn't be a bad thing now, would it"? Eric said.

"Nope, it wouldn't be a bad thing at all," Mike said as he pulled out his note tablet to help prepare Eric's action steps. "Let's figure out what you need to do on your ambulance ride.

Eric began to list them out:

1.   Confirm what really makes me happy so I'm not going to burn out.
2.   Develop a vision for my business that enrolls and inspires not only myself, but my team as well.
3.   Refine my mission statement.
4.   Develop my BHAG (Big Hairy Audacious Goal) for the business.
5.   Figure out my three-year to five-year goals, one-year goals, and 90-day plans.
6.   Begin consistent and never-ending injections of hope-ium into my mind.

Now it's your turn. List all of the things that you need to do in your business to figure out where it's going and put a plan to get it there. Your business may be different than Eric's truck-repair business, so your challenges will be unique to you. Put down what you will do, when you will do it, and who will help you accomplish the task.

Task	By When	Who Will help you
1.		
2.		
3.		
4.		
5.		
6.		
7.		
8.		
9.		
10.		
11.		
12.		
13.		
14.		
15.		
16.		
17.		
18.		
19		
20.		

Chapter
7

Emergency Room-
Letting Your Business Doctors
Stabilize You

The bright, midwinter sun beamed down on Kennewick that almost balmy late January afternoon as Mike pulled into the Clearwater Truck Maintenance and Repair parking lot. A high desert heat wave had enveloped the region and brought a respite of unseasonably warm weather that melted the snow, and allowed the winter-weary population to participate in their favorite spring activities, including golf. As was his habit, whenever his favorite golf course opened up, Mike was sure to be there to play the first round of the year. Normally, that would have been the first week of March, but Mike couldn't pass up this climatically orchestrated good fortune that had befallen the area. He moved his appointments to take advantage of this outdoor opportunity. For the first time, he came to see Eric near the end of the day.

As Mike walked into the facility, he noticed the activity level was much higher than it had been in the past. The team seemed to move with more speed and purpose. All in all, it looked like life was coming back to Clearwater Truck Maintenance and Repair. Mike noticed the mission statement on a wall outside of Eric's office, and as he entered the office, he noticed Eric's new vision statement. Eric was sitting behind his desk, still looking as tired and exhausted has he had ever been.

"Hey, it's starting to look pretty good out there in the repair bays," Mike said with a smile on his face. "I got your financial reports, and it looks like you had your biggest month in the past year. Must feel pretty good, eh?"

"Yes, it sure does," Eric said with a slight smile on his face. "I wish I could just enjoy it more."

"Tell me what you mean by that?" Mike asked.

"You know what, I'm just not really sure," Eric said looking up at his ceiling. "I got my 90-day plan in place, and the team is stoked about the new vision and mission. I've been injecting hope-ium on an almost hour-by-hour basis, and it sure seems to be really helping out."

"What seems to be the struggle?" Mike asked.

"Sometimes, I feel the weight of the world on my shoulders, and I just can't seem to get it off. Even though my leadership team has really stepped up to the plate and taken a lot more day-to-day control of the business, it's always ultimately up to me to make every important decision. I always seem to struggle with that. I just don't feel like I have all the answers and I question some of the decisions I have made. I worry that they might come back to haunt me."

"It's obvious what your problem is," Mike said.

"What's that?" Eric asked

"You are trying to perform first aid on yourself."

"Come again," Eric asked. "What do you mean by that?"

"Your business has been stabilized. You have taken your ambulance ride and figured out what direction you're going, and now you are in the emergency room of business. Now it's time for your doctors, so to speak, to work on you and get you ready for your future business surgery or physical therapy. However, it seems like you're trying to pretend that you don't need your doctors and are doing everything yourself."

"By doctors, you mean business advisors, correct?" Eric asked.

"Yes, and I'm wondering why you're avoiding using them."

"Simple. I'm not bleeding to death any more, but I still have to watch every penny that comes in and goes out of this place. I'm still barely breaking even. I look at how much a lawyer, accountant, or any other advisor would cost, and I just can't justify the expense when I have to make payroll and pay my vendors in order just to keep this place going."

"And how's that working for you?" Mike asked.

Why you can't perform first aid on yourself?

"There you go, sounding like Dr. Phil again," Eric said as he shook his head, not knowing what to say.

"I know how it's working for you Eric. It's not," Mike said. "You went into business with a brilliant knowledge of how to fix trucks, and it's carried you this far. But it's time to acknowledge that you don't know what you don't know. If you had a brilliant legal mind, you'd be making great legal decisions. If you were a great accountant, you would do your own tax planning and never pay one cent more in taxes than you need to. And if you were a genius insurance agent, you would never have too much or too little coverage, and you'd know when and how to review your coverage."

"Ok, so let's concede that I don't know a lot about those things," Eric countered. "What would stop me from taking a few classes on all those topics so I could get smart enough to make my own decisions and not be reliant on all these professionals?"

"Tell me right now when you're going to find the time to take these classes?" Mike responded. "Your free time should be all about pursuing the things that you want to do. Let's be honest, Eric. I don't see you as the type who would tolerate sitting in tax-law classes and getting a lot out of it."

"Yeah, you're probably right. I've never been academically inclined. Let me ask you this: If I did have all this knowledge in these various areas, why would I still need business advisors in the first place?"

"Because this is your business, and you would be prone to making decisions based on your own biased perspective."

"What do you mean by that?" Eric asked

"Have you ever seen ugly kids?"

"Uhhh, yes," Eric asked sort of confused

"Would your kid be one of them?"

"Not a chance," Eric replied as he gestured to the pictures of his kids on his desk. "Look at my kids; they're the cutest things you have ever seen."

"Could somebody else say that they were ugly?"

"They'd be out of their minds," Eric retorted. "And if they did say that, I might just beat the hell out of them."

"You see," Mike said, "you see your kids differently than anybody else would see your kids. You don't look at them objectively because they are your flesh and blood. You could never see them as anything but beautiful since you have so much emotion wrapped up into them. You see your business with a similar view."

"Not sure I'm getting you, Mike."

"You have a lot of emotion wrapped up in your business. Since you have this emotion, making rational decisions is not always the easiest thing to do. Let's go back to your kids. Have you maybe overreacted at times when your kids did something wrong?"

"Yeah, of course."

"So, you might overreact and make an emotion-based decision about your business," Mike answered.

"Ok, I can see where you're going with this," Eric responded. "I need outside expert advisors to help me make rational decisions instead of going off on emotional tangents."

"Or let your Uncle Bob give you business advice." Mike said.

"Yeah, he was never the brightest bulb in the bunch," Eric said as he laughed. "He was trying to get me to run an ad in Inland Northwest Mother Baby that was never going to work."

"Why was he trying to do that?" Mike asked.

"His daughter, Zelda, my cousin, was an advertising salesperson for them, and was going to get me a screaming good deal," Eric laughed as he got out a paper and pad of paper.

"Are you ready to learn about how to select your advisor group?" Mike asked as he laughed along with Eric.

"Let's get busy," Eric said.

What to look for in your advisor team?

Accountant

- Will meet with you personally at least once a year or quarter, depending on your needs.
- Has a game plan for helping you grow the business and not just reviewing numbers. More focused on helping you achieve what you want to get out of your business instead of just strictly focusing on reducing taxes.
- Is willing to meet and work with your other advisors.
- Offers more than just basic accounting. Provides other services such as QuickBooks training and support, payroll services and bookkeeping.
- Emphasis on following the tax laws and not exploring gray areas.

Lawyer

- If possible, will bill as you go or offer a small retainer as you go. Large retainers are a red flag.
- General practitioners are good, but depending on the type of law you are looking at, a specialist is a must in this category.
- Firms are quite often a bad way to go. Too many lawyers wasting your retainer. Go with a solo practice when possible.

Enrolled Agent

- Was previously an IRS agent.
- Understands state law in the state in which they are practicing. Has the ability to represent you in front of state tax authorities.
- Will not shy away from asking you tough questions about your taxes no matter how embarrassing they are.
- Tells you the truth about what you face, and does not candy coat it.
- Tough as nails with IRS and other tax authorities. Will not back down.

Insurance Broker

- Big thing here again is that they can handle multiple services. Business (including employee benefits), personal, life, accidental, death, and so on.
- Independent brokers are best as long as they are backed by AAA-rated companies that are either national with some staying power, or well regarded regional companies with a track record of success and stability.
- Early on, make an assessment as to how much they educate you versus selling you products.
- Must do an annual review with you, with the focus on changes that have occurred in the business and coverage that needs to be increased or reduced.

Banker

- Wants to get to know you.
- Asks a lot of questions about your business and how they can help. Looks for products and services that will benefit your business, even if they are not provided by the bank.
- Demonstrates pro-active communication with you. Will personally call you before a problem occurs with your account.
- Wants to be a partner and assist you with meeting people in the community who could possibly benefit your business.
- No preference for private or public banks. It's all about the people, not the institution.

Business Coach

- Proven track record in jobs and as a coach.
- Testimonials of wins. Knows how to get clients results in their business.
- A clear plan of attack. Does not coach just to solve today's problems.
- Creates effective processes that can be used with a given business. The coach is not just coaching off the top of his or her head.
- Multiple plans for different types of clients. No

one-size-fits-all approach.
- The ability to customize what to do based on needs and not a rigid system that must be followed.

Marketing Expert
- Understands branding/marketing and how to attract your target audience.
- Understands social media and can advise on the best platforms to use and how to use them.
- Can develop print, radio, TV, and other campaigns that would fit your market.
- Has a laser-like focus on return on investment (ROI) and helps you measure that. Does not focus on branding strategies unless it drives real prospects into your business.

Human Resources
- Understands hiring and legal issues revolving around your employees.
- Has a proven track-record of keeping companies out of HR trouble. (Workman's comp claims, legal issues, etc.)
- Uses comprehensive systems in working with clients. Does not reinvent the wheel over and over.

Web Design
- Provides creative work. Combines the artistic with the ability to produce practical layouts specifically geared towards your business. Can create a website that is attractive while addressing functionality issues, is easy to navigate and industry specific.
- Has positive testimonials, especially from clients who have proven lead generation success due to the success of the website. Pretty websites still need to make money.
- Does not treat deadlines with disregard. Is will ing to put together and stick to a timeline and enforces consequences for missing deadlines.
- Works with your marketing person to maximize SEO.

"In general, all of your advisors need to be good listeners, have the ability to think outside the box, care for your business by finding ways to help your business, and be willing to refer your business to individuals and other businesses who could use your services and products."

"That's quite a list of things I should be looking for in advisors," Eric said. "Anything else that is important in this area?"

Your role in working with them

"Eric, the biggest thing you have to be aware of is your own role in working with your circle of advisors. This is not a one-way street. In medicine, I can only be as good as the information I am given. It's impossible for me to make a good diagnosis if the patient hides vital information and symptoms, such as a family history of heart trouble or an addiction to drugs."

"To be honest, I'm afraid of airing out all of my dirty laundry to people I barely know," Eric admitted.

"I know how it might feel especially in the beginning, that's why you need to find people you can trust. Check their references, and do some research on them before you make a decision to work with them. In the end, you have to put aside any bit of shame or embarrassment about your lack of knowledge or mistakes you have made in the past. A good professional will never judge you, never insult you, and never treat you as any less than the professional business owner that you are."

"Ok, got it," Eric said.

"Now remember, in the end, they work for you. If they don't show a high level of professionalism and service, don't hesitate to find someone else…and fast. Don't ever let any of your professionals get away with not working in your best interest, all the way from showing up on time for appointments to correct billing. Their support staffs should also treat you like the respected, valued customer you are to their firm."

"I am assuming that my homework until our next session is

strictly to identify my business doctors, interview them, select them, and then start letting them help me stabilize my business."

"That's right," Mike said. "It's one of the biggest and most important tasks that you will tackle on your business first-aid journey, but in the end, it will also be one of your most rewarding."

"Where do I find them?" Eric asked.

"Referrals. Start with asking people you trust the most. Then talk with business owners within your industry and ask them whom they trust with their business. If that does not produce the individuals you are looking for, start doing some research with an industry-advocacy group, your local chamber of commerce, and finally try doing some research online. Make sure that they have the knowledge, skill, and reputation to help you."

"Ok, guess it's time to get to work," Eric said

"Yes it is," Mike said as he left Eric's office with a big smile knowing that his job was almost done.

Now it's your turn. Begin by identifying your own business doctors who will help you stabilize your business. If you already have a professional helping you out in an area, list that person below and write down what more they need to do to help you in your business. If you don't already have someone in mind for a specific category; create a timeline for when you will have them on board in your business, along with what areas they can help you with.

Business Doctor	Name	Company	Where Can They Help
1. Accountant			
2. Lawyer			
3. Enrolled Agent			
4. Insurance Broker			
5. Banker			
6. Business Coach			
7. Marketing/Ad			
8. Human Resources			
9. Web Design			
10. _____			
11. _____			
12. _____			
13. _____			
14. _____			
15. _____			
16. _____			
17. _____			
18. _____			
19. _____			
20. _____			

Chapter

8

Business Physical Therapy –
Going From
Wounded to Well

Spring on the Columbia River is a spectacular mix of flowering trees, fresh desert grasses, and boats coming out of their winter hibernation. Soon, the parks would be full of families taking their kids for swims, and the river full of wheat barges as they would take their golden treasure down to Portland to be shipped all over the world. On that beautiful April morning, Mike drove down Highway 240 next to the river as he traveled to Eric's shop. It was a bittersweet moment for him as his mind replayed the previous nine months of his quest to help take Clearwater Truck Maintenance and Repair from almost certain termination to business survival. He knew that this was probably his last visit to Eric's business, at least in the role of business coach. Mike's services were constantly in demand, and he always recognized that his role was that of "The Business Doctor." He loved saving businesses from the brink and getting them stabilized so that they had a great chance of success in the future, which was a blessed outgrowth of his skills and desires as an accomplished emergency room doctor. However, Mike knew that in order for Eric to achieve real success in business, he would need to have business physical therapy with a business coach whose job would be to help Eric and his business refine their business practices in order to ensure long-term profitability and success.

Letting go of a client was never easy for Mike, but it was especially difficult in this case as Mike had poured his heart and soul into helping Eric get control of his business. The months had brought conflict, disappointment, and tension as Eric struggled to allow the process to happen. But in the end, the success had been far greater than Mike could have ever expected, and he had developed a great friendship with Eric. Nevertheless, Mike knew that this was the day that he had to break the news to Eric, and tell him that his time with Clearwater Truck Maintenance and Repair had come to an end. Mike plastered on a forced smile as he walked through the front door and through the familiar repair bays on his way to Eric's office. He noticed a whole bunch of trucks with familiar logos, logos he had not seen in the shop in months.

"Hey Doc, you sure look happy this morning," Eric said as he came out of his office to meet Mike.

"Just great to see another spring day," Mike said. "This place sure looks like it's hopping, and do I see what I think see out in the bays?"

"If you mean all those Pendleton Trucks being repaired, that's right," Eric said with a big grin. "I got a call from Jim last week. He heard about my turn around. His new repair company had missed some pretty obvious things that needed to be fixed, which had cost him thousands of dollars in missed deliveries, so he's giving me a second chance. As you can tell, I am making the best of it."

"Wow, that is incredible," Mike said as he scanned the line of vehicles. "I am so excited to see this happening."

"Yeah, but I still have such a long way to go to get this place where I want it," Eric said as he also looked out over the trucks. "I'm still barely breaking even. I know I'm working too many hours, and we still have some dropped balls and team members who don't want to buy into the hope-ium, and..."

"But nothing." Mike interrupted. "This is your time to give yourself a big pat on the back and celebrate how far you've come. Where were you nine months ago?"

"About as low as a man can get," Eric answered.

"That's right. What you have accomplished in such a short period of time deserves recognition."

"So what are we working on today, Doc?" Eric asked as they walked into his office.

Letting go of control

"Eric, it's time for you to start giving more control over to others within your organization and begin by taking some steps back so that all decisions don't have to come from you."

"I thought we dealt with this when we went over my time challenges," Eric said, somewhat incredulously. "You told me not to be such a control freak and delegate tasks to others, and I think I've done a pretty good job with delegating to others."

"Yes you have," Mike answered. "But this is not what I am talking about. I'm talking about decision making and who has authority to make higher level decisions in your business."

"Well, since this is my business, shouldn't I be making the high-level decisions?"

"Of course you should, but how active are you in soliciting input and advice from your trusted managers who have helped you keep this place going over the years?"

"I haven't, because they've never had the knowledge to assist me with that kind of decision making."

"And whose fault is that?" Mike asked.

"I guess it's mine," Eric answered somewhat sheepishly. "I never figured it was in their abilities to understand the things I understood, so I didn't want to rely on them. I just found it easier to make the decision and then tell them what to do."

"Do you think it might be time to start opening the knowledge vault and start sharing that knowledge with your leadership team?" Mike asked.

"I see exactly where you're going with this," Eric said. "I guess it's time to start opening myself up to my leadership team and letting them in on the decision making process. But my concern is...what if they make wrong decisions?"

"So what?" Mike answered with a shrug. "You've made some pretty stupid decisions in this business, and you've survived. Did you learn from those stupid decisions?"

"Yeah, I learned what not to do," Eric answered.

"And so will your leaders," Mike answered. "Think about this, when your kids were babies, did they walk on their first few attempts?"

"No, they kept falling down over and over again."

"If you had walked for them, do you think they would have struggled to learn how to walk on their own?"

"Are you saying that my managers and leaders are like babies, and I haven't let them walk?" Eric asked.

"Does the shoe fit?" Mike asked in return.

"Yeah, and I guess I've been wearing it for all these years," Eric answered. "What do I do about it?"

"Start looking at all the decisions that you make every day, week, month, and year. What are decisions that you can let your team leaders make without potentially disastrous results? If you are the one who decides the brand of toilet paper, let someone else decide. If you have been the decision maker on marketing strategies, let someone else decide. If the decision works out, great; if it doesn't, get them to learn from their mistakes and get them back in the decision making game."

"That's going to take a lot of time working with them to get them to that decision making level. What if I sink all that time and energy into training them and they keep making mistakes?"

"What is your alternative?" Mike asked.

"I don't know," Eric answered, "but what if I train them to be great managers, and they leave me for my competition? Then what?"

"Let me ask you this," Mike answered leaning right up to Eric. "What if you don't train them, and they stay?"

"Ouch," Eric answered with a pained expression. "Ok, you got me. It's time to start training my leadership team to walk on its own. Come to think about it, I probably should have started this years ago."

"And in the end, your stress level will end up being much less precisely because others you trust are making major decisions on your behalf. Your duty is to make sure those decisions are evaluated, measured, and used as teachable moments for your team."

"Next week, I will sit down with my leadership team and start assigning decision making responsibilities just as you recommended," Eric answered as he wrote furiously in the notebook he had started carrying around with him.

Business practices for a lifetime

"Eric, let's go over some things I'd like you to focus on. These are business practices that will serve you for a lifetime. Some of these will deal with your personal life, but they will have a direct impact on your business life. Let's go over them."

1. Make sure you pay yourself first and foremost. Working for free becomes demoralizing after awhile, and besides, that's not why you went into business. Yes, it's good to sacrifice yourself for the sake of the business, but long-term martyrdom will never energize you to take a business to new heights. Remember what you're told by the flight attendants on safety briefings before your plane takes off. Put your oxygen mask on first, and then put it on your children. You can't assist others if you are unconscious.

2. Find a way to quantify as many things as possible in your business. You cannot grow what you cannot measure. Find a way to quantify everything from financial performance right down to how well your vendors take care of you.

3. Get rid of cancerous employees. Negative, self-serving employees are a drain on your business. It does n't matter how skilled they are, or what level of respect they have with others inside or outside the business. You have to get rid of them. Nobody is indispensable in a business, so make the hard call and show them the door. The others on the team will thank you for your tough minded. courageous leadership.

4. Work on catching employees doing things right. When you focus on negativity, you develop fearful employees who will hide things from you. The more you point out their successes, the more they will want to do things that please you.

5.	Send thank you notes every day to people who have given to you. Develop an attitude of gratitude. Focus on what you have and be thankful instead of focusing on what you don't have. Sending a note to those people who have given to you opens you up to more and more blessings in your life.

6.	Treat your vendors as your business partners. Your vendors who provide goods and services to your business are just as invested, or even more invested, in your success than your customers. Their success is dependent upon your success, so let them help you with ideas and suggestions to make your business better. Closing yourself off to them or treating them as less-than-equals does nothing for your eventual success

7.	Get in shape. If you are tired all the time, take a look at your exercise routine, or lack thereof. Walking from your desk to the front reception area does not count as an exercise routine. Start with walking three nights per week, and then build up from there.

8.	Candy bars and donuts are not primary food groups. A steady diet of junk food isn't doing anything for your business future or your overall health. The fact that you work hard is no excuse not to eat well. Bring a balanced lunch to work and keep fruit available for snacks. Almonds are one of the best afternoon snacks out there.

9.	Yes, even you have time to go to the doctor and dentist. Business owners are notorious for avoiding medical appointments. However, missing work for weeks with a heart attack or preventable medical issues because you were too busy to see a doctor is one of the dumbest things you can do. Yes, I'm talking to you. Make that annual physical appointment today.

10.	Get a life! If you live, eat, and breathe your business, pretty soon it will overwhelm you. Nurturing your personal relationships with those you love and care about will do more for you than any of the above nine elements combined. Nobody ever said on their deathbed 'Gee, I wish I had spent more time at work.' Find a way to leave your business at the end of the day and focus on the truly important things in your life.

Having a Business Coach for a lifetime

"I agree those are all great principles, but frankly, Mike, it isn't easy to focus on all of those when you have to tackle the day-to-day principles of life. When I'm in the trenches of my business on a daily basis, sometimes I'm going to have bad dietary habits, and I won't always remember to write thank-you notes."

"And that's why you need a business coach for a lifetime in your business," Mike responded.

"You are my business coach," Eric said, somewhat perplexed.

"Eric, I know that this is difficult for you. When you and I started with each other, you knew that my role as your business doctor was to help you apply first aid to your business. You have done a wonderful job and now you are on the road to recovery. Frankly, my services as a business doctor have grown in demand as more and more businesses suffer life-threatening circumstances. It's time for you to go to the next stage of your recovery, and for that, you will need a business coach who can give you true business physical therapy."

"To be honest, this isn't easy for me to hear," Eric responded with disappointment in his voice. "I have entrusted you with everything that goes on in this business, and I just don't know how I'm going to trust anyone else to that degree."

"Eric, I have an excellent business coach that I will have you talk to...someone who I know will take good care of you. He has proven himself over and over again with hundreds of businesses and I have complete faith in him to take good care of you."

"Why do I need a business coach for a lifetime?" Eric asked. "That just seems expensive and unnecessary, especially as my business improves and I can handle everything on my own."

"Let me ask you this Eric. What is your favorite sports team?" Mike asked.

"You know that I'm a big Seattle Seahawks fan," Eric answered.

"Will they always have a coach?" Mike asked.

"Well of course they will."

"So if successful sports teams will always have a coach to lead them to success, why wouldn't a business also have a coach for a lifetime?"

"Ok, that makes some sense, so what's the role of a business coach for me?" Eric asked.

"Your coach will make you do those things I just mentioned. Just like a sports coach makes you do exercises that you don't want to do, your business coach will get you to stick to a plan for continuous business improvement. The fact is that without accountability, it will be very easy to regress into your bad habits...the ones that got you here in the first place. We've done too much work over the past nine months for it to all come unraveled because you think you've got it made."

"Ok, you're right. It's been easy for me over the years to think I've got it made, when in fact I've deluded myself into a false reality. I certainly don't want to go there again," Eric responded. "So when should I expect the call from the Coach?"

"I'll have him give you a call tomorrow," Mike responded. "Bringing him on board will be the best decision you'll ever make."

"No Mike, having you come into my life has been the best decision I've ever made," Eric responded, his eyes welling up with tears and his voice brimming over with emotion and gratitude.

"Thank you for your belief in me, and thank you for never giving up, even when it seemed hopeless," Mike said warmly.

Mike gave Eric a big bear hug, then turned around and walked out of Clearwater Truck Maintenance and Repair for the last time. He knew that a new future was about to begin for Eric and his business, a future full of hard work and some struggles, but nevertheless a future full of success, joy, and prosperity.

As Mike walked out the door, Eric looked around his desk and saw the divorce papers lying there. "I wonder if it's possible to restore my family as I continue to restore my business?"

18

IMPORTANT QUESTIONS

*How ActionCOACH
Can Take Your Business
Over the Top!*

1. So, who is ActionCOACH?

ActionCOACH is the world's #1 business coaching firm, originated in 1993 by founder and CEO Brad Sugars,

ActionCOACH is the fastest growing company of its kind in the world, with offices and Business Coaches from Singapore to Sydney to San Francisco. From the beginning, **ActionCOACH** has been set up with you, the business owner, in mind.

As an alternative to conventional and costly consulting firms, **Action-COACH** is designed to give you both short-term assistance and long-term training through its affordable and effective mentoring approaches.

After years of workshops, group coaching sessions and one-on-one coaching programs focused on our exclusive business building strategies, **ActionCOACH** has attracted more than 10,000 clients and more than 500,000 seminar attendees who will attest to the power of our programs.

Based on proven sales, marketing, and business management systems, **ActionCOACH** not only shows you how to increase your business revenues and profits (often quite dramatically), but also how to develop your business so that as the owner, you can work less, relax more and enjoy business ownership.

Our Business Coaches have substantial business experience, and are fellow business owners who have invested their time, money and energy to make their own various business ventures successful.

Your success truly does define our success!

2. And, why do I need a Business Coach?

Every great performer, whether an athlete, a business owner or an entertainer, is surrounded by coaches or advisors. As the world of business moves faster and becomes increasingly more competitive, it's difficult to keep up with all the changes in your industry, in addition to running your business every day.

Just like great athletes find success by following the lead of a coach with a winning game plan, more business owners than ever before are turning to Business Coaches to help develop a winning game plan for their businesses.

Why? First of all, it's very difficult to be truly objective about yourself. A Business Coach can be objective for you, and can see the "forest for the trees."

A sports coach will make you focus on the game and will make you run more laps than you like. A good coach will also tell it like it is and will give you small pointers about the game and your competition. A great coach will listen and guide you to success.

Likewise, a Business Coach will make you focus on your business and hold you accountable to the things you should do in relation to where you want your business to be. A good Business Coach will also become your marketing manager, your sales director, your training coordinator, your partner, your confidant, your mentor and above all else, your best friend. Most importantly, your **ActionCOACH** will help you make your dreams come true.

3. What's an Alignment Consultation?

Great question. The Alignment Consultation is the point where an **ActionCOACH** begins the process with every business owner.

Your investment includes a 2 to 3 hour meeting with your **ActionCOACH**. During this meeting your **ActionCOACH** will learn as much as possible about your business, your goals, your challenges, your sales, your marketing, your finances and so much more.

Everything is approached with 3 main goals in mind. First, to know exactly where your business is now. Second, to clarify your business and personal goals. And third, to get the crucial pieces of information needed to create an **ActionPLAN** for your business over the next 12-months.

The plan isn't a traditional business or marketing plan, but rather a step-by-step plan of Action you'll work through as you continue through the duration of our one-on-one coaching program...

4. So, what is one-on-one coaching?

Simply put, it's one of our most popular programs, and it's the only program in which your **ActionCOACH** will work with you one-on-one for a full 12-month cycle to make all of your goals a reality.

From weekly coaching calls and goal setting sessions to creating your new marketing pieces, you will develop new sales strategies and business systems so you can work less and learn all you need to know to make your dreams come true.

Your monthly investment ensures that your **ActionCOACH** will dedicate a minimum of 5 hours a month to work with you on your sales, marketing, team building, business development and every element of the **ActionPLAN** you created during your Alignment Consultation.

Unlike a consultant, your personal **ActionCOACH** will do more than just show you what to do; he or she will actually be with you when you need them most. Your **ActionCOACH** is there for you as each idea takes shape, as each campaign is put into place, as you need the little pointers to make things happen. Your **ActionCOACH** will also be there when you need someone to talk to, when you're faced with challenges, or most importantly, when you're just not sure what to do next.

Your ActionCOACH will be there every step of the way.

5. Why at least 12-months?

If you've been in business for more than a few weeks, you've seen at least one or two so-called "quick fixes". Most consultants seem to think they can solve all your problems in a few hours or a few days.

At **ActionCOACH**, we believe long-term success means not just doing it for you; it means doing it with you, showing you how to do it, working alongside you and creating success together.

Over the course of 12-months, you'll work on different areas of your business. Each month, you'll not only see your goals become a reality, you'll gain both the confidence and the knowledge to make it happen again and again-- even when your first 12-months of coaching is over.

6. How can you be sure this will work in my industry and in my business?

ActionCOACH is expert in the areas of sales, marketing, business development, business management, and team building, and with literally hundreds of different profit-building strategies, you'll soon see how truly powerful our systemized approaches are.

Because you are the expert in your business and industry, together we can apply our systems to make your business more effective.

Because of our network of more than 1,000 offices around the world, there is not a business, industry or category our Business Coaches haven't either worked with, managed, worked in or even owned that isn't the same or very similar to yours.

Our extensive network means when you hire an **ActionCOACH**, you hire the full resources of the entire **ActionCOACH** team to find a solution for any and every challenge you may have. Imagine hiring a company with the collective knowledge of hundreds of experts ready to help you.

7. Won't this just mean more work?

Of course, when you set the plan with your **ActionCOACH**, it may seem a bit overwhelming, but no one ever said attaining your goals would be easy. In the first few months, it will take some work to adjust to your new plans, but the further you work into the program, the less work you'll actually have to do. You will, however, be amazed at how focused you'll be and how much you'll get done.

8. How will I find the time?

Again, the first few months will be the toughest, not because of an extra workload, but because of how differently you'll work. In fact, your **ActionCOACH** will show you how, on a day-to-day basis, to get more work done with much less effort.
In other words, after the first few months you'll find that you're not working more, just working differently. Then, depending on your

goals, from about month six onwards, you'll start to see the results of all your work. At this point, if you choose, you can start working less than ever before. Just remember, it's about changing what you do with your time...NOT putting in more time.

9. How much will all this cost?

Your investment will depend on the size of your business and the scope of our undertaking together. Your **ActionCOACH** will work this out with you so it will be appropriate for your business and the goals you want to achieve.

You'll find that having an **ActionCOACH** is just like having a marketing manager, sales team leader, trainer, recruitment specialist and con-sultant-- all for one nominal investment.

Everything you do with your personal **ActionCOACH** is truly an invest-ment in your future. Not only will you begin to create great results within your business, but you'll end up with an entrepreneurial edu-cation that is second-to-none. With that knowledge, you'll be able to repeat your business success over and over again in other ven-tures.

10. Will it cost me extra to implement the strategies?

Again, give your **ActionCOACH** just a half-hour and you'll be shown how to turn your marketing into an investment that yields sales and profits rather than just running up your expenses. We have a system that works. We know how to achieve our goals and can now leave our business and go on lengthy holidays.

In most cases, an **ActionCOACH** will actually save you money when that coach discovers areas that aren't working for you or your busi-ness. For some marketing programs, you will need to spend some money to make some money. Yet, when you follow our simple testing and measuring systems, you'll never risk more than a small expendi-ture on each campaign. And when we find the campaigns that work, we make sure you keep profiting from them time and again... Remember, when you default to the accounting way of saving costs, you can only add a few percentage points to your bottom line, how-ever, by following the ActionCOACH formulas, your returns from your sales and marketing can be exponential.

11. Are there any guarantees?

Yes! As the leading coaching company in the world, we are also the only coaching company of any kind to guarantee our work, and to guarantee that you will get results!

Remember, though we're still your Business Coach and we can't do your work for you. You're still the major player, and it will always be up to you to take the field and perform. We will push you, cajole you, help you, be there for you, and even do some things with you … but in the end you've still got to do the work. Ultimately, only YOU can ever be truly accountable and responsible for your own success.

We will guarantee to provide the best service and support available, to answer your questions and challenges promptly, and to offer you the most current and appropriate processes and approaches.

Finally, we are fully committed to helping you become successful, whether you like it at the time or not. Once we've helped you set your goals and create your plan, we'll do whatever it takes to make sure that you achieve your goals while at the same time promoting a balanced lifestyle as an overriding theme in all we do.

This is to ensure that you never compromise either the long-term health and success of you or your company, or your own personal core values and what's most important to you.

12. What results have other business owners seen?

Everything from owners previously working 60 hours a week down to working just 10, through revenue increases of 100 to even 1,000 percent. Our results speak for themselves, and are highlighted by specific examples featuring real people with real businesses getting really great results.
There are three main reasons why this will work for you and your business. First, your **ActionCOACH** will help you get 100% focused on your goals and the step-by-step processes to get you there. This focus alone is amazing in its effect on you and your business results.

Second, your **ActionCOACH** will hold you accountable for getting things done, not just the day-to-day running of the business, but for the dynamic growth of the business. You're making an investment in your success-- and we're going to get you there.

Third, your **ActionCOACH** is going to teach you as many of our proven328 profit building strategies as you may need.

So, whether your goal is to make more money, work fewer hours, or both; within a period of the next 12-months your goals can become a reality.

But don't take our word for it. Just ask any of the thousands of existing **ActionCOACH** clients, check out the results on our website or ask your **ActionCOACH** for a copy of our global testimonial DVD "Action Speaks Louder Than Words."

13. What areas will you coach me in?

We will work with you in five key areas ... and the emphasis for each will depend on you, your business, and of course, your goals.

These key areas are:

• *Sales*-- The backbone for creating a profitable business, and one of the areas we'll help you get spectacular results in.

• *Marketing & Advertising*-- If you want to make a sale, you've first got to find a prospect.

Over the next 12 months your **ActionCOACH** will teach you the amazingly simple, yet powerful, streetwise marketing techniques and approaches that will drive profits.

• *Team Building & Recruitment*-- You'll never just "wish" to find the right people again. You'll have motivated, passionate, enthusiastic, and loyal team members for your business when your **ActionCOACH** shows you how.

• *Systems & Business Development*-- End the hopeless cycle of "the business running you" and begin running your business. We will show you the secrets of having your business "work" even when you're not there.

• *Customer Service*-- Discover how to deliver your product or service consistently, making it easy for your customers to buy and leaving them feeling delighted with your service. Learn new ways to motivate your current customers to give you referrals and to ensure their repeat business. These are just two of the many strategies we will teach you.

14. Can you also train my people?

Yes. In fact, we believe that training your people is almost as important as coaching you.

Your **ActionCOACH** can provide you and your business with many different training modules, including **TeamRICH, SalesRICH, PhoneRICH** and **ServiceRICH**. You'll be amazed at how much enthusiasm and commitment comes from your team as they experience each of our training programs.

15. Can you write ads, letters and marketing pieces for me?

Yes. Your **ActionCOACH** can do it for you. Your **ActionCOACH** can also train you to do it yourself, or simply critique the marketing pieces you're using right now.

Should you want us to handle it for you, you won't get just one piece. We'll design several for you to take to market and test which one is the best performer. If it's just a critique you're after, we'll work through your piece and offer feedback in terms of what to change, how to change it and what else you should do to make it effective. Finally, we can recommend a variety of books or resource materials which provide a "home study" opportunity for you so you'll know how to do it yourself next time.

16. Why do you also recommend books and DVDs?

We do this to save you both time and money. You can learn the basics in your own time, so when we do get together we'll be working on higher level implementations rather than the basics.

It's also a very powerful way for you to speed up the coaching process and get *phenomenal*—as opposed to just great results.

17. When is the best time to get started?

Right now! Before you take another step, waste another dollar, lose another sale, work too many extra hours, miss another family event, or forget another special occasion. You need to call **ActionCOACH** today.

Far too many business people wait and see, mistaken in thinking that working harder will make everything better. Remember, what you know got you where you are today. So how's that working for you? To get where you want to go, you've got to make some changes and most likely, you'll have to learn something new.

There's no time like the present to get started on your dreams and goals.

18. So, how do we get started?

First, you need to get back in touch with your **ActionCOACH**. There's some very simple paperwork to sign and you're on your way! Next, you'll need to invest a few hours showing your coach everything possible about your business.

Together you'll create a plan--and then the work really starts! Remember, it may seem like a big job in the beginning, but with an **ActionCOACH**, you're sharing the load.

Together, we'll achieve great things!

RESOURCES & REFERENCES

Customer Service Resources

Customer Satisfaction is Worthless, Customer Loyalty is Priceless – Jeffrey Gitomer

Give 'Em The Pickle – Bob Farrell

Survey Monkey -www.surveymonkey.com

Tax Help and Representation Resurces

National Association of Enrolled Agents - www.naea.org

Time Management Resources

First Things First – Steven Covey

7 Habits of Highly Effective People - Steven Covey

E-Mail Marketing Resources

Constant Contact – www.constantcontact.com

STORM – www.spokanerainmaker.com

Business Planning Resources

Mastering the Rockefeller Habits - Verne Harnish

Business Coaching Resources

ActionCOACH Business Coaching – www.actioncoach.com or www.actioncoachspokane.com

Branding/Marketing Resources

Beautiful Media – www.beautimedia.com

Recommended Reading List:

Instant Cash Flow – Brad Sugars

The Business Coach – Brad Sugars

The E-Myth Revisited – Michael Gerber

Purple Cow – Seth Godin

Guerrilla Marketing – Jay Conrad Levinson

The 22 Immutable Laws of Marketing – Al Ries & Jack Trout

The One Minute Manager – Ken Blanchard & Spencer Johnson

QBQ! The Question behind the Question – John G. Miller

Awesomely Simple – John Spence

The 21 Irrefutable Laws of Leadership – John Maxwell

The Little Red Book of Sales – Jeffrey Gitomer

Crush It! – Gary Vaynerchuk

Rich Dad Poor Dad – Robert Kiyosaki

Think and Grow Rich – Napoleon Hill

The Answer – John Assaraf & Murray Smith

Who – Geoff Smart & Randy Street

Delivering Happiness – Tony Hsieh